EVERYDAY CROCHET

the complete beginner's guide

June Gilbank

Contents

Flecked **Scarf**

pg. 216

Three Simple **Washcloths**

pg. 64

Puff Stitch **Scarf**

pg. 176

Triangle **Bunting**

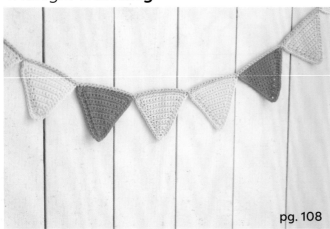

pg. 108

Circular **Coasters**

pg. 126

Pretty **Headband**

pg. 164

Cozy **Cowl**

pg. 220

Colorblock **Potholder**

pg. 98

Handy **Baskets**

pg. 228

Front-and-Back **Fingerless Mitts**

pg. 254

Solid Stripes **Bag**

pg. 240

Rolling Waves **Blanket**

pg. 236

Double Diagonals **Shawl**

pg. 246

Front-and-Back **Hat**

pg. 250

Phone or Tablet **Slipcover**

pg. 224

Placemat and **Coaster Set**

pg. 232

Introduction

Ever since I started creating and publishing my crochet designs at PlanetJune (planetjune.com), I've loved discovering and sharing new things about my craft with others. For me, the best thing about crochet is its versatility. It's pretty amazing that with just a hook and a ball of yarn, you can combine a few simple stitches into infinite shapes and textures. From those, you can crochet a huge variety of items—from blankets and toys to garments and accessories.

How to Use This Book

Even if you've never before taken hook to yarn, you can learn how to crochet. In these pages, I teach you how, starting from the very basics, with tons of tips for making the learning process easier. Lots of close-up photos guide you through every stitch and technique. For complete beginners, I've created the clearest, most comprehensive learn-to-crochet tutorials. For those looking to improve their skills, I've distilled all the knowledge and tips I've picked up over my crocheting life into these pages. To help you put into practice everything you've learned, I've also included a collection of fun and stylish patterns—I hope you try them all!

Learning to crochet shouldn't be a struggle but rather an easy, fun, gradual progression that builds from absolute basics—and that's what I set out to create with *Everyday Crochet*.

This is the book I wish I'd been given when I was learning to crochet and I hope you'll find it a valuable resource—whether your goal is to learn to crochet, improve your crochet know-how, or find fabulous new designs to crochet.

If you're new to crochet, I recommend you work through Part 1 page by page. Then, as you learn more techniques with each new chapter, try out the practice projects to put what you've learned into action. If you get stuck at any point, flip back for a quick refresher or make use of the helpful appendixes at the end of the book to find what you're looking for. With each chapter, project, and pattern, you'll learn something new you can take forward into your future crocheting—and grow in skill level and confidence.

As you follow along with the lessons in this book, starting with the most basic stitches as you crochet your first simple (but useful!) washcloth, you'll be building skills so you can crochet beautiful hats, scarves, bags, lacy shawls, and more—armed with nothing more than your trusty crochet hook and a ball of yarn!

Acknowledgments

Knit Picks graciously provided all the beautiful yarn used in this book and my bamboo-handled Susan Bates crochet hooks are courtesy of Coats & Clark.

Thank you to my wonderful team at DK for all their work helping make this book the best it can be. Thanks to Stacey Winklepleck at Knit Picks and Catherine Babbie and Cynthia Schnall at Coats & Clark for their kind assistance. I'd like to thank my mum, Lilian Linden, for beta-testing all my instructions from a noncrocheter's perspective, and my husband, Dave, for patiently listening to me talk crochet for hours on end and for always believing in me. Thank you to all my family and friends who've offered advice and support and for understanding when I had to go incommunicado to meet my deadlines. Thanks to all my readers and customers who allow me to continue to live the dream as a professional crochet designer and especially to the members of the PlanetJune online community—it's a privilege to be the figurehead of such a warm, friendly, and enthusiastic crochet-loving community.

I hope you enjoy this book as much as I've enjoyed creating it for you!

About the Author

June Gilbank is an accomplished crochet pattern designer, writer, blogger, and multi-crafter. June taught herself to crochet when she moved from the United Kingdom to Canada in 2003, and she's since designed and published hundreds of unique nature-inspired crochet patterns at PlanetJune (www.planetjune.com). Her specialties are cute and realistic animal, plant, and seasonal amigurumi designs as well as elegant accessories that showcase the beauty and variety of crochet.

June studied science and math at university and has worked as a technical writer. She uses these skills on a daily basis to bring clarity and precision to her crochet patterns and tutorials.

June is the author of *Idiot's Guides: Crochet*, *The Complete Idiot's Guide to Amigurumi*, and *Paper Chains & Garlands* as well as the ebooks *The Complete Guide to Giant Amigurumi* and *The Punchneedle Handbook*. She occasionally contributes articles and patterns to other books and magazines.

When she isn't crocheting, June enjoys exploring wildlife and nature, trying new crafts, and cozying up at home in Ontario, Canada, with her husband, Dave, and their dog, Maggie.

PART 1
The Basics

CHAPTER 1

Before You Begin

Choosing Your Yarn

One of the many nice things about crochet is the wide variety of yarns you can work with. However, with so many choices, it can be overwhelming!

So which yarn should you use, especially when you're new to crochet? A smooth yarn that feels good in your hands is the best choice when you're just starting. Choose a plain, soft yarn in a color you love, but avoid very dark colors at first. Your stitches will show more clearly with lighter-colored yarn. Novelty yarns with loops, bobbles, fluff, or glitter might be tempting right now, but they're more difficult to work with because the texture obscures your stitches. Wait until you have a thorough grasp of the basics of crochet before you attempt to work with one of these yarns.

Whatever yarn you choose, it will likely come wound in a skein, ball, or hank, most often with a paper ball band surrounding it. The ball band contains useful information about the yarn, including its weight, fiber composition, yardage, care instructions, and more.

You can crochet using the yarn tail found on the outside of the skein or fish out the tail from the middle of the skein (a center-pull skein). Some higher-end yarn is packaged in a *hank*—a large loop of yarn twisted into a coil. To avoid tangles when you crochet with a hank, undo the twisted coil and hand-wind the yarn into a ball or use a yarn winder to wind it into a center-pull skein.

Yarn Weights

The weight of a yarn refers to its thickness, not the weight of a ball or skein. Yarn varies in thickness from very thin lace weight (which you can crochet gossamer-fine shawls with) to super bulky (which is more suited for thick blankets and oversized chunky scarves) and every thickness in between. Lighter yarns need smaller hooks and take more stitches and rows to produce the same-sized piece of crocheted fabric you'd get with a heavier yarn paired with a larger hook.

When you're just beginning to learn to crochet, a medium-weight yarn is a good choice. Perfect for a wide range of projects, it's thick enough that you can easily see your stitches. Look for a *worsted weight yarn*. Depending on the manufacturer, it could also be called *medium*, *#4*, *aran*, or *10-ply*.

Yarn Fibers

Yarn can be made from plant fibers (such as cotton, linen, and bamboo), animal fibers (such as wool, alpaca, mohair, and angora), and man-made fibers (such as acrylic, nylon, and microfiber).

Cotton is strong, inelastic, and absorbent, which makes it a good choice for kitchen and bathroom items, such as dishcloths and washcloths. *Mercerized cotton* has been processed to make it strong, smooth, and shiny, but it's also less absorbent.

Wool is light and stretchy and makes warm winter clothes. Check the care instructions carefully; most wool shrinks when washed. *Superwash wool* has been treated so it can be machine washed without the fibers felting or binding together.

Acrylic is inexpensive and easy to care for, but it can't tolerate heat. It's often available in a wide range of colors that make it particularly suitable for blankets and toys.

Yarn can also be produced from a blend of fibers, which combines the properties of each. For example, acrylic can be added to cotton to give it some stretch or added to wool to make it washable.

How Much Yarn Do You Need?

When crocheting from a pattern, you need to know how much yarn to buy. Each pattern tells you approximately how much length (yardage) of which weight of yarn is required to complete the project, so look for a yarn that's the same weight and check the ball band for the yardage. Calculate how many balls of yarn you need by dividing the yardage specified in the pattern by the yardage of 1 ball and rounding up to the nearest whole number.

Yarn is dyed in batches, all of which have slight color variances from other batches. To be sure all the yarn you buy is exactly the same shade, check each ball band to ensure every ball comes from the same numbered dye lot.

All About Crochet Hooks

Crochet hooks are available in a range of sizes, materials, and styles. A good hook feels comfortable in your hand and helps you form stitches without difficulty. With time and experimentation, you'll find the type of hook that works best for you and your crocheting style.

Hook Anatomy

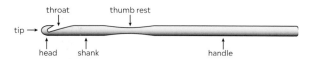

A crochet hook is made of a few basic parts: the tip, throat, shank, head, thumb rest, and handle. A pointier **tip** can get into tight stitches more easily, while a more rounded tip is less likely to split the yarn. The **throat** catches the yarn and the **shank** holds your working loops and determines your stitch size. The shape of the **head** varies by manufacturer. *In-line* hooks have the head directly in line with and the same size as the shank, whereas *tapered* hooks have a more curved shape and a narrower throat.

The **thumb rest** helps you control and rotate the hook and the **handle** helps balance the hook while you crochet. If you have large hands, you might find a longer handle more comfortable. If holding a crochet hook is uncomfortable for you, try a hook with a cushioned or shaped handle.

Hook Sizes

The size of your hook, measured by the width across the shank, determines the size of the stitches you create. The hook size you need is related to the thickness of the yarn you choose: Thicker yarns require larger hooks.

Crochet hooks are labeled in either U.S. or metric sizes or both. U.S. sizes are characterized by letters and/or numbers and the equivalent metric measurement is given in millimeters, as shown in the following table. Note that the U.S. letter/number size labels can vary among brands. If in doubt, check the metric size—it's less ambiguous.

For thread crochet, fine steel hooks are available in a range of very small sizes, numbered from U.S. 00 to 14 (decreasing from 3.5 to 0.75mm).

U.S. Size	Metric Size
B/1	2mm, 2.25mm
C/2	2.5mm, 2.75mm
D/3	3mm, 3.25mm
E/4	3.5mm
F/5	3.75mm, 4mm
G/6	4mm, 4.25mm
G/7	4.5mm
H/8	5mm
I/9	5.5mm
J/10	6mm
K/10.5	6.5mm, 7mm
L/11	8mm
M, N/13	9mm
N, P/15	10mm

When you're starting out, it's best to use a medium hook size (and a medium weight yarn) so the hook is easy to hold and maneuver and your stitches are large enough to see clearly. For your first hook, a U.S. H/8 (5mm) or U.S. I/9 (5.5mm) is a good choice.

Hook Materials

Crochet hooks are commonly made from metal or plastic, but you can also find hooks made from wood or bamboo.

Aluminum is smooth, strong, and long-lasting, but it might feel cold and inflexible in your hands.

Wood feels warm and flexible, but it needs to be well finished so it doesn't have any rough spots that will snag yarn and conditioned so it doesn't dry out.

Plastic is smooth and inexpensive, but it makes a squeaky noise when used with some yarns and can bend or break relatively easily.

Bamboo is lightweight and flexible, but it's prone to splintering or snapping, especially in smaller sizes.

Each material has pros and cons, and you might want to try a couple to see which you prefer before you invest in multiple sizes.

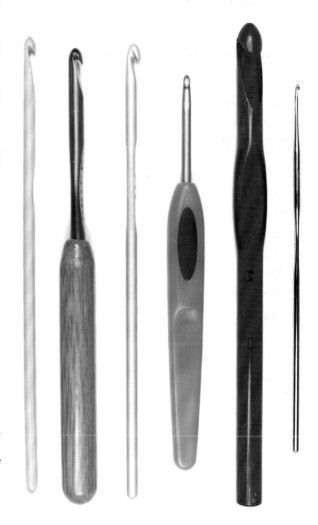

The Tools You Need

One of the joys of crochet is its portability. You really only need a hook, a ball of yarn, and maybe a pattern—and you're ready to go. However, a few more tools can make things easier.

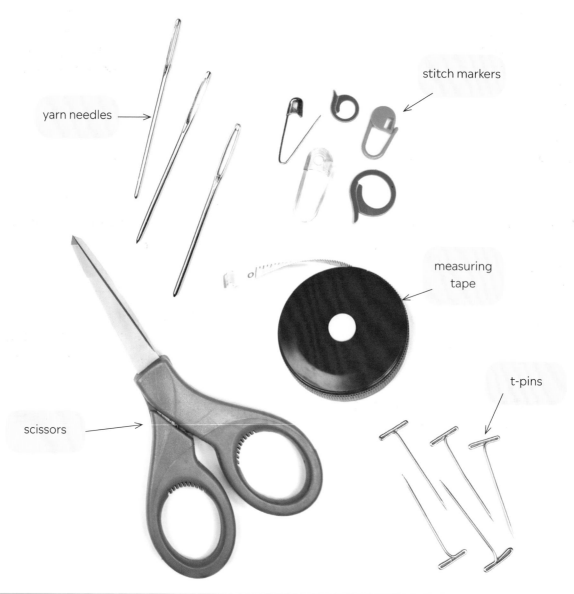

yarn needles

stitch markers

measuring tape

scissors

t-pins

Essential Tools

Scissors are an essential tool for crochet. You'll use them to cut the yarn at the end of each piece and to trim yarn tails when you finish your work. A small, sharp pair is best to make clean, accurate cuts.

You'll need a **yarn needle** (also called a *tapestry needle* or *darning needle*) to weave in your yarn tails and stitch pieces together. Yarn needles are thick and blunt-tipped and have a large eye to fit the yarn into. Metal needles are preferable; plastic needles bend easily and can snap.

A **measuring tape** (or ruler) is invaluable for checking your gauge and the size of your finished pieces. A retractable measuring tape is a good addition to your crochet kit. It's small and portable, and you never know when it might come in handy.

Stitch markers have multiple uses. You can use them to mark specific stitches in your crochet so you don't lose your place in a pattern, and more importantly, you can place a stitch marker in your working loop to save your work from unraveling when you put down your crochet.

Pins are essential if you're going to block your crochet. T-pins are a good choice. They're long, sturdy, and easy to handle. Be sure to choose rustproof pins so you don't end up with rust stains ruining your handiwork.

Other Helpful Tools

A **row counter** is useful if you're likely to get distracted or you're working on a large piece. Just remember to advance the counter at the end of each row and you'll never lose your place.

A **case** keeps all your crochet tools together. You don't need anything fancy. Your essentials should fit nicely into a pencil case or small makeup bag. When you develop a collection of different hooks, you can store them on your desk in a pen cup or organize them by size in a roll-up fabric case with a pocket for each hook.

Take care when shopping for stitch markers. Ring-shaped stitch markers are only used for knitting; crochet stitch markers must have an opening so you can remove them when you're done with them. Plastic split-ring markers, locking stitch markers, and coil-free safety pins are all good choices. In a pinch, you can also use a scrap of yarn or a bobby pin as a marker.

Holding Your Hook and Yarn

There's no single correct method for holding your crochet hook and yarn. With time, you'll discover the method that works best for you. The most important thing is that you're comfortable. If you feel any discomfort or pain, try a different hold or position until you find one that feels natural to you.

Holding Your Hook

The two most common ways to hold a crochet hook are the *overhand* (or *knife*) grip and the *underhand* or (*pencil*) grip. For either grip, grasp the hook's thumb rest between the thumb and index finger of your right hand so the throat of the hook faces you.

For the knife grip, place your hand over the hook and support the handle against your palm with your remaining fingers, as if you're holding a knife.

For the pencil grip, let the handle of the hook rest on top of your hand, as if you're holding a pencil.

Holding Your Yarn

Your left hand also plays an important part in your crocheting: It controls the tension in your yarn, which influences how tight your stitches are. You can wrap the yarn over and around your fingers in any number of ways. Here are two of the most common.

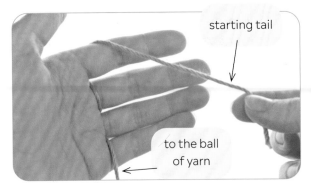

starting tail

to the ball
of yarn

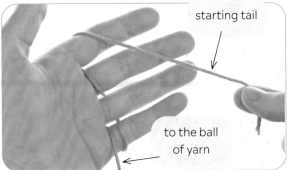

starting tail

to the ball
of yarn

With your left palm facing you and the end of the yarn in your right hand, pass the yarn in front of your little finger, behind your ring finger, in front of your middle finger, and behind your index finger.

With your left palm facing you and the end of the yarn in your right hand, bring the yarn over and around your little finger in a complete loop and then pass the yarn behind your ring finger, in front of your middle finger, and behind your index finger.

Your left hand will stay busy as you crochet. You'll also hold your work steady between your left thumb and middle finger.

Whichever option you choose, when you have the yarn wrapped through your fingers, close your hand gently around the yarn so your palm faces down. The yarn should be able to slide through your fingers without chafing your hand but not so freely that the working yarn goes slack. Keeping the yarn taut as you work helps keep your stitches neat and even.

Crochet For Left-Handers

Although most crochet patterns and tutorials assume a right-handed crocheter, the good news is that all crochet patterns and all instructions written in this book are also applicable to left-handers—with only four substitutions, as shown in the following table. See the Left-Handed Reference (starting on page 258) for complete left-handed instructions for everything you need to start crocheting as a left-hander.

When this is what the photo shows for a right-hander ...

Every Time You See ...	Replace It With ...
Right	Left
Left	Right
Clockwise	Counterclockwise
Counterclockwise	Clockwise

To follow the right-handed photos in any crochet book or pattern, you can hold them up to a mirror. The reflection will show each photo from a left-handed perspective.

Left-handed crochet produces a mirror image of the same article made by a right-hander. This means that almost all crochet patterns are perfectly fine for left-handers to use without making any changes to the pattern. Any diagonal details will slant the opposite way and spirals will rotate in the opposite direction, but that rarely presents a problem.

this is what you'd do if you're left-handed.

The only times you have to be careful are when the left and right sides of a piece aren't interchangeable. For example, if you follow a colorwork pattern involving text, the letters would all be back to front unless you start the chart at the end of each row and work backward. A cardigan pattern would give you buttonholes and buttons on the wrong sides unless you make changes to the pattern directions.

When you read a crochet chart, every other row will also be backward for right-handers, so it's no more difficult for lefties to interpret a chart than it is for righties.

This swatch was stitched by a left-handed crocheter.

First Steps

Making a Slipknot

To begin crocheting, you need to attach your yarn to your hook with a slipknot.

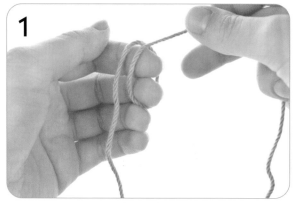

Leaving a 6-inch (15cm) tail of yarn hanging down over your left hand, lay the yarn over one or two fingertips and take it around them to form a loop.

Remove your fingers from the loop, holding it in place between your thumb and a fingertip, and insert your hook into the loop.

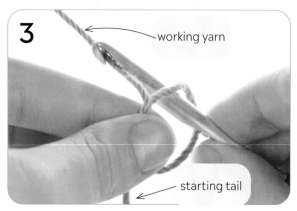

Catch the working yarn with your hook. (The working yarn is the yarn that heads to the yarn ball, not the short starting tail.)

Use the hook to pull the yarn up through the loop.

5

Pull on the yarn ends to tighten the knot.

6

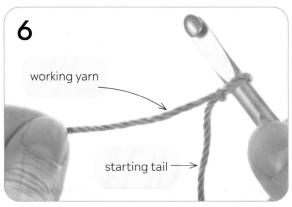

working yarn

starting tail →

Pull the working yarn to draw the loop closed around your hook.

7

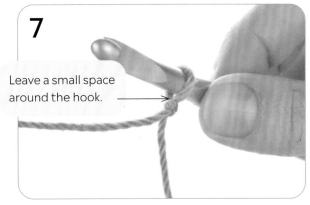

Leave a small space around the hook. ←

Leave the loop loose enough that your hook can easily slide up and down inside it.

If you find you need to pull on the starting tail instead of the working yarn to tighten the slipknot around your hook, you've made an adjustable slipknot (a knot that can loosen itself). You need a secure knot to start your crochet, so if you've accidentally made an adjustable slipknot, undo it and start again.

Making a Yarn Over

A *yarn over* (YO) is one of the most essential moves in crochet. Although it might sound like you wrap the yarn around the hook with your left hand, it's quicker and easier to keep your left hand still and use your hook to grab the yarn.

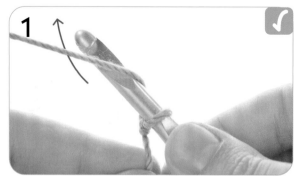

Pass your hook underneath the yarn so the yarn lies over the hook. The working yarn (that heads to your left hand) is on the left side of the hook.

Do not pass the hook over the yarn and catch it from above so the working yarn is on the right side of the hook. This would twist your stitches.

To yarn over twice, swing the hook over and back under the yarn again in the same direction.

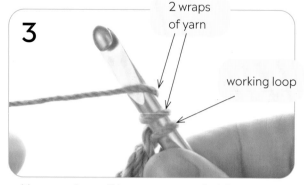

2 wraps of yarn

working loop

You now have 3 loops on your hook: the working loop and the yarn wrapped twice around the hook.

Drawing Up a Loop

All crochet stitches are formed by inserting your hook into a previous stitch and pulling a new loop through that stitch. This process is called *drawing up a loop*.

Insert your hook into the next stitch.

Yarn over. To draw up a loop, reverse the path of your hook so you pull the hook back out of the stitch, drawing the yarn with it.

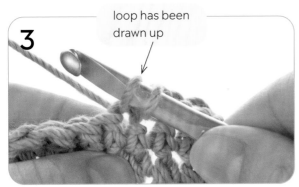

loop has been drawn up

The loop you've drawn up is now on your hook, along with the loop you started with.

If you see "insert hook in next stitch and draw up a loop" or "draw up a loop in the next stitch" written in a pattern, that means the yarn over is implied. You can't draw up a loop without first catching the yarn with your hook.

Making a Foundation Chain

The *foundation chain* runs along the bottom of your crocheted piece and provides a base into which you work your stitches.

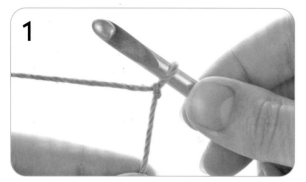

Start with a slipknot on your hook.

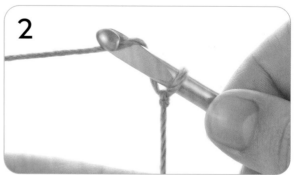

Yarn over.

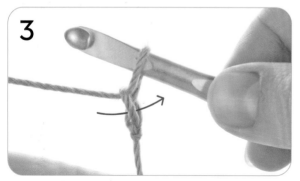

Draw your hook back through the loop already on your hook.

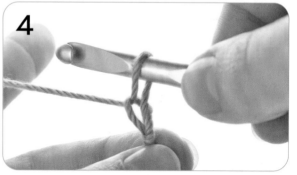

You now have 1 chain (abbreviated *ch*).

To make it easier to draw the yarn through your stitches, rotate the hook toward you after you yarn over. With the head of the hook facing sideways, it's less likely to catch on your stitches.

5

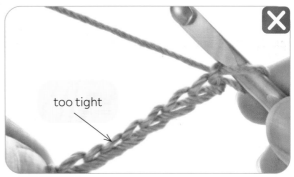

too tight

Repeat steps 2 and 3 for each additional chain. To help support the chain as you pull your hook through, hold on to the stitches you've already chained with your left hand. Move your hand up the chain every few stitches so you always hold the chain close to your hook.

It will take some practice to make your chains look consistent. Although a loose chain might look untidy, resist the urge to neaten your chain stitches by pulling on the yarn to shrink the stitch. This would tighten the stitch into a knot, which isn't what you want. A crocheted chain must be loose and open so you can insert your hook back into each chain loop without a struggle.

Counting Chains

If you look at your chain, the front of the chain—the side that faces you as you crochet—should look like a row of Vs. Each of these Vs is one chain stitch. When you count your chains, start from the V above the slipknot and count each V up to your hook. The loop on your hook is called the *working loop*. **Do not** count this as a stitch.

To make it easier to keep count when you're making a long foundation chain, mark every 10 or 20 chains with a stitch marker.

If in doubt, especially with a long starting chain, add a few extra chains to ensure you have enough. You can easily unravel the extras after you complete the first row if you have too many. However, if you have too few, you'd have to unravel the entire first row to add the additional chains.

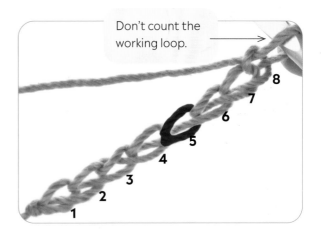

Don't count the working loop.

Working into the Foundation Chain

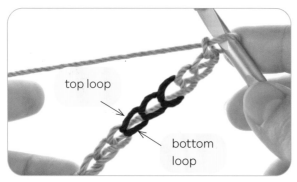

Look at the front side of your foundation chain and you'll see it looks like a row of sideways Vs. Each V is made of two loops: the *top loop* and the *bottom loop*.

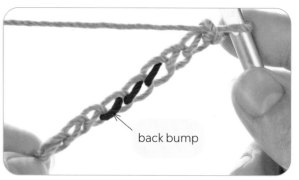

If you turn over the foundation chain, you'll see a line of bumps along the back. These are called the *back bumps* of the chain.

There's no one correct way to insert your hook into a chain. The most important thing is to be consistent and insert your hook into the same part of the chain to begin each stitch. The following sections show the most common ways to work into a chain.

Under the Top Loop

In this method, you hook under the top loop only.

Here, the hook is inserted under the top loop only.

Under the Top Loop and Back Bump

In this method, you hook under both the top loop and the back bump. This is sometimes referred to as the *top 2 loops* of the chain.

Here, the hook is inserted under the top loop and the back bump.

Under the Back Bump

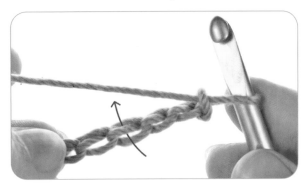

In this method, you turn over the chain and insert your hook under the back bump of each chain.

Here, the chain has been turned over and the hook is inserted under the back bump.

Which should you use? Working into the top loop only is the easiest method for beginners and the way the stitches in this book are made unless otherwise noted, but it makes a loose edge with large holes. After you've gained some confidence with making crochet stitches, I recommend working into the back bumps of the chain (unless a pattern specifies otherwise) because it makes a strong, neat edge. The stitch demonstrations in Chapter 3 are all worked in the easiest way: into the top loop of the chain.

Working into Subsequent Rows

Standard crochet stitches are worked from right to left, so when you reach the end of a row, you turn your work so you can work from right to left across the top of the row you just completed.

Before turning your work, you'll make a *turning chain* to bring your hook and yarn up to the height of the next row. The number of stitches in your turning chain depends on the stitches you're making. (See "Turning Chains" on page 48 for more details.)

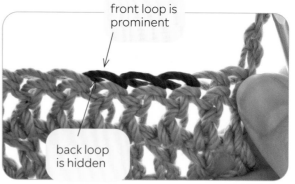

After turning your work, look at the top of the row you've just completed. The top of each stitch looks like a sideways V—similar to the front of a chain stitch. Each V is made of two loops: the *front loop* (the loop closest to you) and the *back loop* (the loop farthest from you).

You'll need to tilt your work forward to clearly see the Vs along the top of the row. If you look straight at your work from the front (as shown above), you'll only see the front loops of the stitches because the back loops are lower and farther back.

Under the Front and Back Loops

Unless otherwise specified in a pattern, the standard way to work into a crochet stitch is by inserting your hook under the front and back loops of the stitch in the previous row.

Here, the hook is inserted under the front and back loops.

Under the Front Loops Only

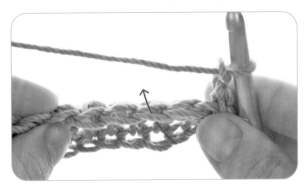

If a pattern specifies that your stitches are worked in *front loops only*, insert your hook under just the front loop.

Here, the hook is inserted into only the front loop of the stitch.

Under the Back Loops Only

If a pattern specifies that your stitches are worked in *back loops only*, insert your hook under just the back loop.

Here, the hook is inserted into only the back loop of the stitch.

If a pattern doesn't specify which loop(s) to work into, insert your hook under both loops of the stitch below. If you work into only one loop, the unworked loops form a horizontal ridge along the base of every row.

CHAPTER 3

Common Stitches

Single Crochet

Single crochet (abbreviated *sc*) is the most basic crochet stitch—and the easiest one to learn.

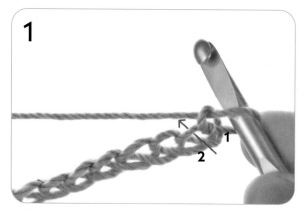

Make a foundation chain of the required number of stitches plus 1. Identify the second chain from your hook.

Insert your hook into the second chain from your hook and yarn over.

Draw up a loop. This leaves you with 2 loops on your hook.

Yarn over and draw the yarn through both loops on the hook to complete the stitch. This leaves you with 1 loop on your hook.

5

Complete the first row of single crochet stitches by repeating steps 2 through 4 into each remaining chain. At the end of the row, chain 1.

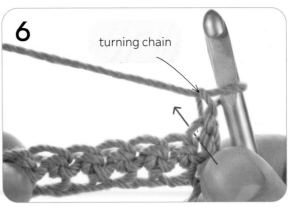

6

turning chain

Turn your work and identify the first stitch of the row.

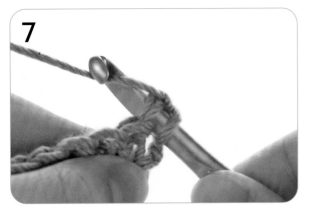

7

Insert your hook under both loops of the stitch and yarn over.

8

Repeat steps 3 and 4 to complete the stitch.

At the end of each row of sc, remember that the turning chain ***does not*** count as a stitch. Don't stitch into it or your work will get one stitch wider with every row.

Double Crochet

Double crochet (abbreviated *dc*) is another common stitch. It's double the height of the single crochet stitch.

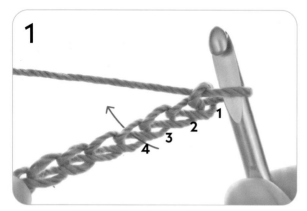

Make a foundation chain of the required number of stitches plus 2. Identify the fourth chain from your hook.

Yarn over and insert your hook into the fourth chain from the hook.

Yarn over and draw up a loop. This leaves you with 3 loops on your hook.

Yarn over and draw the yarn through 2 loops on the hook. This leaves you with 2 loops on your hook.

5

Yarn over and draw the yarn through both loops on the hook to complete the stitch. This leaves you with 1 loop on your hook.

6

Complete the first row of double crochet stitches by repeating steps 2 through 5 into each remaining chain. At the end of the row, chain 3.

7

Turn your work and identify the second stitch of the row. Remember, the turning chain counts as the first stitch, so don't work into that stitch.

8

Yarn over and insert your hook under both loops of the stitch. Repeat steps 3 through 5 to complete the stitch.

At the end of each row of dc, remember that the turning chain from the row below counts as a stitch. You must make the last dc stitch into the top of the turning chain or your work will get one stitch narrower with every row.

Half Double Crochet

Half double crochet (abbreviated *hdc*) is halfway between the two most common stitches—single crochet and double crochet—in height.

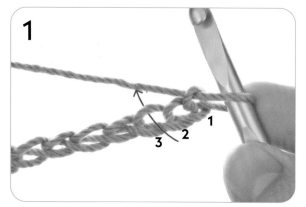

Make a foundation chain of the required number of stitches plus 1. Identify the third chain from your hook.

Yarn over and insert your hook into the third chain from your hook.

Yarn over and draw up a loop. This leaves you with 3 loops on your hook.

Yarn over and draw the yarn through all 3 loops on the hook to complete the stitch. This leaves you with 1 loop on your hook.

5

Complete the first row of half double crochet stitches by repeating steps 2 through 4 into each remaining chain. At the end of the row, chain 2.

6

Turn your work and identify the second stitch of the row. The turning chain counts as the first stitch, so don't work into that stitch.

7

Yarn over and insert your hook under both loops of the stitch.

8

Repeat steps 3 and 4 to complete the stitch.

At the end of each row of hdc, remember that the turning chain from the row below counts as a stitch. You must make the last hdc stitch into the top of the turning chain or your work will get one stitch narrower with every row. The turning chain is particularly easy to miss with hdc stitches, so pay close attention at the end of each row.

Triple (Treble) Crochet

Triple crochet (abbreviated *tr*) is also commonly referred to as *treble crochet*. This stitch is the tallest of the basic stitches, at about 3 times as tall as a single crochet.

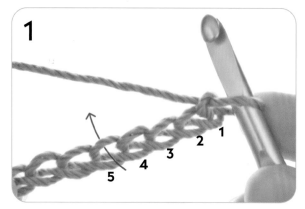

Make a foundation chain of the required number of stitches plus 3. Identify the fifth chain from your hook. The first 4 chains count as your first stitch.

two yarn overs

Yarn over twice and insert your hook into the fifth chain from your hook.

Yarn over and draw up a loop. This leaves you with 4 loops on your hook.

Yarn over and draw the yarn through 2 loops on the hook. This leaves you with 3 loops on your hook.

5

Yarn over and draw the yarn through 2 loops on the hook. This leaves you with 2 loops on your hook.

6

Yarn over and draw the yarn through both loops on the hook to complete the stitch. This leaves you with 1 loop on your hook.

7

Complete the first row of triple (treble) crochet stitches by repeating steps 2 through 6 into each remaining chain. At the end of the row, chain 4, turn your work, and identify the second stitch of the row. The turning chain counts as the first stitch, so don't work into that stitch.

8

Yarn over twice and insert your hook under both loops of the stitch. Repeat steps 3 through 6 to complete the stitch.

At the end of each row of tr, remember that the turning chain from the row below counts as a stitch. You must make the last tr stitch into the top of the turning chain or your work will get one stitch narrower with every row.

Turning Chains

Before you start crocheting subsequent rows beyond your foundation row, you need to make a chain to get your hook and yarn up to the height of the next row. This chain is known as a *turning chain*, even in cases where you don't actually turn your work.

Turning Chain Height

The height of the turning chain you need depends on the height of the stitch you're making in the upcoming row. The length of the turning chain depends on how loosely or tightly you make the chain stitches. You might find that—especially for the taller stitches—you need one fewer chain than specified.

If your turning chains bulge out at the edges of your project, try using one fewer chain to see if that gives you a neater edge.

If your turning chains pull your work together at the edges, try using one extra chain to see if that helps straighten the edge.

The following table gives you standard turning chain lengths for the basic stitches.

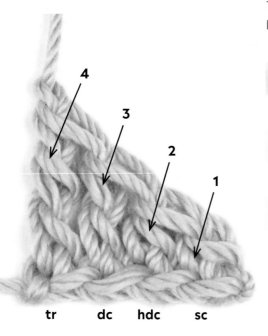

Stitch	Number of Turning Chains
Single crochet (sc)	1
Half double crochet (hdc)	2
Double crochet (dc)	3
Triple (treble) crochet (tr)	4

The Final Stitch

Typically, the turning chain for a single crochet doesn't count as a stitch. However, the turning chain for any taller stitches is used in place of the first stitch of the next row.

If you're following a pattern, it will advise whether the turning chain does or doesn't count as a stitch. If it does count, you'll skip the stitch below the chain and make your next stitch into the following stitch. If it doesn't count, you'll make your first stitch into the final stitch of the previous row, at the base of the chain.

Where the turning chain replaces a stitch, it's vital you remember to work a stitch into the top of the turning chain at the end of the next row.

top of
turning chain

This row might look complete, but it's actually missing the final stitch, which is worked into the top of the turning chain from the row below.

Now the row is complete, with the final stitch at the top of the turning chain. Without this stitch, your work will get narrower with each subsequent row.

Don't worry if you notice a larger gap at the start of each row, between the chain and the next stitch. This is normal. A chain is less bulky than the stitch it replaces, so it always leaves a slight space.

If you still find it difficult to tell where to make your final stitch, here's a technique you can try. You need two stitch markers—one for each end of your work.

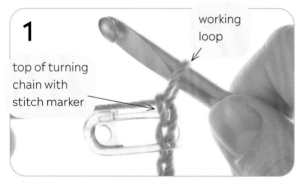

Immediately after making each turning chain, slip a stitch marker into the last chain you made. This is the chain immediately below the working loop on the hook.

At the end of the next row, remove the marker from the top of the turning chain and crochet the final stitch into that chain.

Turning Direction

At the end of a row, you can either turn your work clockwise or counterclockwise before you start the next row. The direction in which you turn the work twists the turning chain one way or the other.

It doesn't matter if you turn clockwise or counterclockwise, but be consistent in whichever direction you choose to give your work a more uniform appearance. Also, you'll find it easier to recognize the top of your turning chain if it looks the same every time you need to work back into it.

You can try crocheting a small sample with a few rows turned clockwise and a few counterclockwise to see which way you prefer. (I find that turning counterclockwise gives me the cleanest result, but the choice is yours.) Then try to stick to that turning direction every time you turn your work in the future.

Slip Stitch

Slip stitch (abbreviated *sl st*) is a stitch with practically no height. It's rarely used as the main stitch to form crocheted fabric. Instead, it's usually used to join stitches at the ends of rounds, connect two pieces, or move the hook and yarn to a new position without adding height.

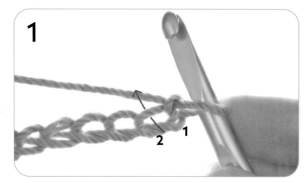

Make a foundation chain of the required number of stitches plus 1. Identify the second chain from your hook.

Insert your hook into the second chain from the hook and yarn over.

Draw up a loop. This leaves you with 2 loops on your hook.

Don't yarn over, but continue to draw the yarn through the remaining loop on the hook to complete the stitch. This leaves you with 1 loop on your hook.

Complete the first row of slip stitches by repeating steps 2 through 4 into each remaining chain. Although you won't usually work more than one row of slip stitches, here's how to continue if you want to go on to a second row.

With practice, you might be able to complete steps 3 and 4 in one fluid motion. However, as you learn, pausing between the steps helps keep your slip stitches from becoming too tight.

5 working yarn

At the end of the row, turn your work clockwise so the working yarn ends up at the back.

6

Identify the first stitch of the row.

7

Slip stitch crochet is usually worked into the front or back loop only, so insert your hook under the loop(s) of the stitch as instructed in your pattern and yarn over.

8

Repeat steps 3 and 4 to complete the stitch.

As with the chain stitch, you form the slip stitch from a single loop of yarn. This means that as you form the next stitch, you'll also pull on the previous stitch, making it shrink. If you need to work back into your slip stitches, keep your tension very relaxed as you crochet so the stitches stay loose.

Easy Finishing

Fixing Mistakes

As you're stitching, if you realize you've made a mistake, it's easy to unravel your stitches to before you went wrong. This is known as *ripping back* or *frogging*.

1 Remove your hook from the working loop and take hold of the working yarn.

2 Pull the yarn and your stitches will unravel one at a time.

3 Continue to pull out your stitches until you reach a point before you made the mistake.

4 To start stitching again, insert your hook into the loop that remains at the end of the previous stitch.

Depending on how many stitches you need to remove to correct your error, you can either carefully count the stitches you unravel so you know where to resume, or you can undo the entire current row, up to and including the turning chain, and start again from scratch.

Fastening Off

Now that you've seen how easy it is to unravel your work, you'll want to prevent that from happening accidentally, so it's important to fasten off securely when you reach the end of your crocheting.

Cut the working yarn, leaving a 6-inch (15cm) tail. Yarn over using the yarn tail.

Pull the tail through the last loop on your hook. Keep pulling until the cut end is drawn through to the top.

Pull the tail tight to close the last loop around the tail.

Your yarn tail should be long enough to weave the end in securely so it will be hidden and won't be visible or pull free—and 6 inches (15cm) is plenty of yarn for that task. If you'll be stitching two pieces together, you can leave a longer tail to use for seaming. Your pattern should specify if you need to leave an extra-long tail. If you forget to leave enough length for seaming, you can cut a new length of yarn to stitch with, but that will leave more ends to weave in later.

Basic Edging

To straighten the sides of your finished piece and make all the edges look the same, you can stitch a border of single crochet all around the edge.

Insert your hook into the stitch at the top-right edge of your piece, draw up a loop of the edging yarn, and ch 1. Starting with the same stitch, sc into each stitch along the top of your project.

When you reach the corner, make 3 sc into the corner stitch. This keeps the corner square and helps it lie flat.

To keep the edge flat, you'll make a different number of sc stitches into the edge of each row depending on the height of the stitches in the row. For sc, work 1 sc into the side of each row. For dc, work 2 sc into the side of each row. For taller or shorter stitches, you'll have to adapt the number of stitches you make. Try to keep the spacing between your stitches as even as you can. If the edging looks wavy or ruffly, you have too many stitches, so space your stitches farther apart or crochet the edging with a smaller hook. If your edging is pulling the surrounding fabric in, you have too few stitches, so space your stitches closer together or crochet the edging with a larger hook.

3

Rotate your work 90 degrees so you can crochet along the side of the piece. To prevent large gaps between the edging and the next stitch, insert your hook *into* the edge stitch (under 1 or 2 loops only), not around the entire stitch.

4

At the next corner, work 3 sc into the corner stitch and rotate your work 90 degrees. Crochet along the bottom of your piece, making 1 stitch into the unworked loop(s) of each stitch of the foundation chain.

5

At the corner, work 3 sc into the corner stitch and rotate your work 90 degrees. Crochet as you did for the first side.

6

At the last corner, work 3 sc into the corner stitch, join with a sl st to the first stitch of the border, and fasten off.

For a neat finish, use the same color for the border as you used for the rest of your project or use a contrasting color to make the border stand out. If your piece has a distinct front and back, crochet the edging with the front (the right side) facing you. This edging can also be used as the base row for other, more decorative edgings. See Chapter 14 for some examples!

Weaving in Ends

Once you've finished crocheting your project, you'll still have yarn tails dangling from where you started, ended, changed color, and/or joined new yarn. It's important to weave in these yarn ends carefully and securely so they don't unravel with use.

Your end weaving should be as unobtrusive as possible, so if your project has a right and wrong side where the wrong side won't be seen, such as a hat or sweater, weave the ends in along the wrong side so they're invisible from the right side. For projects where both sides will be seen, such as a scarf or reversible blanket, take a little extra care to ensure your end weaving doesn't show on either side of the piece. If your piece has more than one color, weave each end through stitches of the same color so it blends into the fabric.

If your yarn is slippery—common with silk, rayon, or bamboo fiber yarns—the ends are more likely to work loose over time. To prevent this, leave extra-long yarn tails—8 inches (20cm) should be plenty—and weave them in different directions. If necessary, you can tack the ends to surrounding stitches with matching sewing thread or use a tiny dab of fabric glue. Do a test to be sure you're satisfied with the look and feel of the end result before using them on your project.

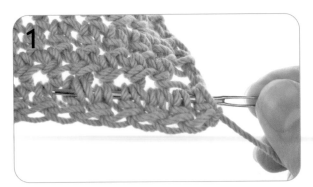

1

Thread the tail through a yarn needle and insert the needle through several stitches. It doesn't matter which direction you choose, but find a path that keeps the needle passing through the middle of your stitches.

2

To avoid adding bulk, don't weave through the same stitches twice.

To weave the tail in securely, change direction after a couple inches and weave back for another inch or so in the opposite direction.

3

When the tail is securely woven in, pull on the fabric in several directions to be sure the tail won't distort the fabric when it's stretched.

4

With a pair of sharp scissors, trim the remaining tail close to your work. Stretch the piece again until any remaining tail is hidden inside the last stitch you wove it through.

Crocheting Over the Ends

You can sometimes avoid weaving in ends altogether by crocheting over them. This works especially well with motifs where you're changing color with every round.

When you start a new yarn or change color, hold the yarn tails along the top of the stitches you'll be working into.

As you crochet, work around the tails so your stitches encase them.

When you've crocheted over sufficient stitches, trim the remaining yarn from the tails. Or for added security, weave the ends back through a few stitches in the opposite direction before you trim them.

Weaving in Too-Short Ends

You should always leave a yarn tail of at least 6 inches (15cm) when you start crocheting and whenever you join new yarn or fasten off so you have sufficient length to properly weave in the ends. If you've accidentally cut a yarn tail too short to weave in, don't despair.

Insert the yarn needle along the path of the end weaving *before* you thread the needle.

When the eye of the needle is close to the short tail, thread the tail through the needle and draw it through the stitches.

Three Simple Washcloths

With this set of pretty and practical washcloths, you can practice your single, half double, and double crochet stitches. Keep them for yourself or give them as gifts.

Basic Measurements

Each washcloth is about 7 inches (18cm) square.

Yarn

About 55 yards (50m) worsted weight cotton or cotton blend. Shown in KnitPicks Dishie, 100% cotton.

Hook

U.S. I/9 (5.5mm)

Other Supplies

Yarn needle, scissors, measuring tape

New Techniques

First Steps (Chapter 2; page 25)

Single Crochet (page 40)

Double Crochet (page 42)

Half Double Crochet (page 44)

Fastening Off (page 57)

Weaving in Ends (page 60)

Single Crochet Washcloth

Leaving a 6-inch (15cm) starting tail, chain 25.

Row 1: Single crochet in the 2nd chain from the hook and in each remaining chain. You should have 24 stitches.

Row 2: Chain 1 and turn your work. Single crochet in each stitch across. Remember that the turning chain doesn't count as a stitch. You should still have 24 stitches.

Repeat Row 2 until your washcloth is square. It should take about 27 to 30 rows. When you get close to the right size, lay the washcloth flat and use a measuring tape to check the width and height. Continue to measure after every row until the height and the width are close.

Fasten off, leaving a 6-inch (15cm) tail. Thread the tail through a yarn needle and weave it into the stitches of the washcloth. Repeat for the starting tail. Snip both yarn ends close to your work.

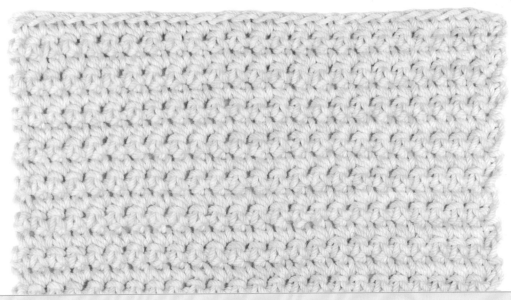

Half Double Crochet Washcloth

Leaving a 6-inch (15cm) starting tail, chain 25.

Row 1: Half double crochet in the 3rd chain from the hook (the first 2 chains count as the first stitch) and in each remaining chain. You should have 24 stitches, including the unworked chains at the beginning.

Row 2: Chain 2 and turn your work. The turning chain counts as the first stitch, so half double crochet in the 2nd stitch and each remaining stitch across. Don't forget to crochet into the turning chain at the end of the row. You should still have 24 stitches, including the turning chain.

Repeat Row 2 until your washcloth is square. It should take about 18 to 20 rows. When you get close to the right size, lay the washcloth flat and use a measuring tape to check the width and height. Continue to measure after every row until the height and width are close.

Fasten off, leaving a 6-inch (15cm) tail. Thread the tail through a yarn needle and weave it into the stitches of the washcloth. Repeat for the starting tail. Snip both yarn ends close to your work.

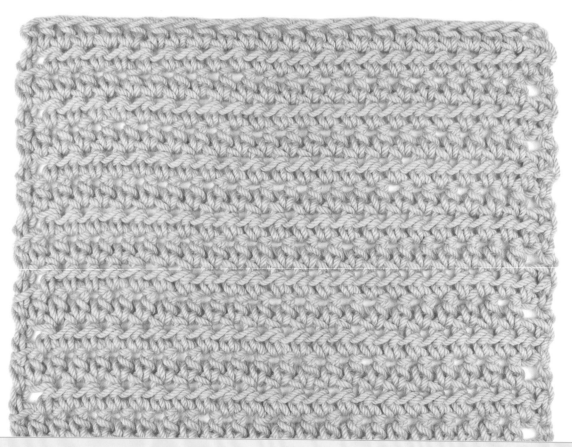

Double Crochet Washcloth

Leaving a 6-inch (15cm) starting tail, chain 26.

Row 1: Double crochet in the 4th chain from the hook (the first 3 chains count as the first stitch) and in each remaining chain. You should have 24 stitches, including the unworked chains at the beginning.

Row 2: Chain 3 and turn your work. The turning chain counts as the first stitch, so double crochet in the 2nd stitch and each remaining stitch across. Don't forget to crochet into the turning chain at the end of the row. You should still have 24 stitches, including the turning chain.

Repeat Row 2 until your washcloth is square. It should take about 13 or 14 rows. When you get close to the right size, lay the washcloth flat and use a measuring tape to check the width and height. Continue to check after every row until the height and width are close.

Fasten off, leaving a 6-inch (15cm) tail. Thread the tail through a yarn needles and weave it into the stitches of the washcloth. Repeat for the starting tail. Snip both yarn ends close to your work.

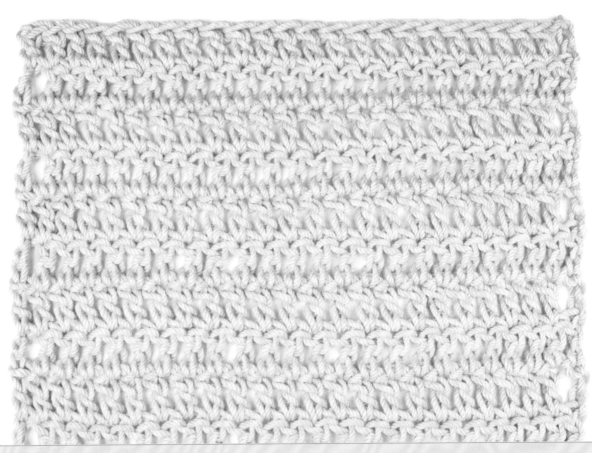

Crochet-Speak

Identifying and Counting Stitches

The best way to spot a mistake in your crochet is to count your stitches. But you have to know what you're looking for among all those loops.

Identifying Stitches

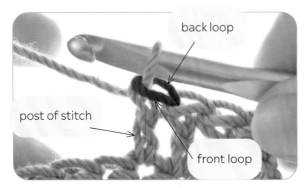

The V at the top of each stitch sits slightly to the right of the post of the stitch.

Think of the V as an arrowhead and the post as the arrow's shaft. The arrow points away from the shaft, so the post sits at the wide end of the V.

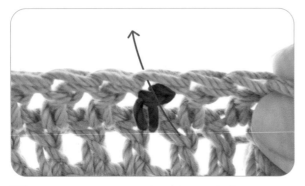

When you turn your work at the end of a row, the Vs from the row below point to the *left*. To work into those stitches, insert your hook into the V that sits slightly to the *left* of the post of the stitch.

If you don't turn your work between rounds, the Vs always point to the *right*. To work into those stitches, insert your hook into the V that sits slightly to the *right* of the post of the stitch.

Counting Stitches

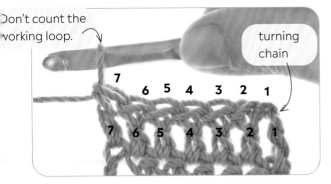

Don't count the working loop.

turning chain

7 6 5 4 3 2 1

7 6 5 4 3 2 1

When counting stitches, you can either count the line of Vs across the top of your work or the posts of the stitches. In either case, take care when you reach the turning chain. If it counts as a stitch in your pattern, don't forget to include it in your stitch count. If you're counting Vs, remember that the working loop on your hook never counts as a stitch.

Counting Rows

For tall stitches, you can clearly see the posts of each stitch. Each post corresponds to one row.

With shorter stitches, like single crochet, the fabric looks very different depending on whether you're working in rows (or turned rounds) or in rounds and not turning your work.

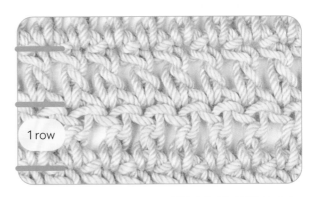

1 row

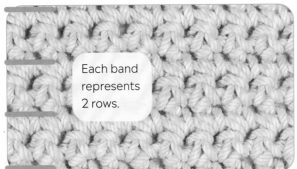

Each band represents 2 rows.

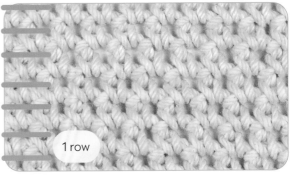

1 row

When you're working single crochet in rows, every other row looks the same because you see the front of the stitches in one row and the back of the stitches in the next. Each distinct band you see is actually formed from *two* rows, so you'll probably find it easier to count the *pairs* of rows rather than individual rows.

When you're working single crochet in rounds without turning, every round looks the same. Each band of stitches corresponds to 1 row.

Gauge (Tension)

Gauge, or *tension*, is a measure of the number of rows and stitches you make per a certain length and width of crocheted fabric. It's usually listed as the number of stitches and rows in a 1-inch (2.5cm) or 4-inch (10cm) sample. The larger the area you have to measure, the more accurate you'll be.

Gauge depends on your hook size and the yarn you use, but it also depends on your style of crocheting and how loose or tight you make your stitches. You might need a hook two or three sizes larger or smaller than another crocheter to make stitches of the same size—even if you use the same yarn and pattern!

Stitching a Swatch

Crocheting a *swatch*—a sample of your pattern—is an easy way to measure the size of your stitches. Using your stitch pattern and the hook and yarn you plan to use for the project, crochet a sample piece. This swatch should be at least 4 inches (10cm) square, not including the edge stitches and rows, which might be distorted and won't give an accurate measurement.

Measuring

To measure your gauge, lay out your swatch flat without stretching it. Place a ruler horizontally on your crocheted fabric, with the 0 mark at least one stitch away from the edge of your swatch. Then count the number of stitches between 0 and 4 inches (10cm). Repeat the process to check your rows, placing the ruler vertically on the fabric and counting the number of rows over 4 inches (10cm).

If the finished item will be blocked, block the swatch in the same way you plan to block the full project before you measure the gauge. Then you'll get a more accurate measurement.

If the number of stitches in your swatch measurement is less than the number of stitches in the gauge statement, your stitches are too large and you need to make another swatch using a smaller hook. If your swatch measurement contains more stitches than what's indicated in the pattern, your stitches are too small and you need to make another swatch using a larger hook. To match the pattern, continue making swatches using larger or smaller hooks as required until you find success.

Is Gauge Critical?

If you're making a garment, you want to be sure it will fit when it's finished, so the gauge is very important. If you don't match what's stated in the pattern, your garment won't fit.

But with many crochet patterns, it might not be that essential. For example, if you're making an accessory, toy, or home décor item, you have more freedom. Do you mind if your scarf or blanket turns out slightly smaller or larger than the pattern dimensions? If not, you don't need to worry much about the size of your stitches. More important is that you like the look and feel of the fabric you're creating.

Drape

The *drape* of a crocheted fabric is how it feels and flows. If you match the pattern but your fabric feels too stiff, firm, or rigid, you might crochet more tightly than the pattern designer or be using a thicker yarn than specified or one with different properties. Using a larger hook means your finished piece will be larger than the pattern specifies, but it will improve the drape.

The looseness or tightness of your stitches might change depending on your stress level. If your stitches have become smaller and more difficult to work into, try to relax your hands and arms and crochet more loosely. Once you get caught up in the rhythm of your crocheting, you'll probably find the repetitive motions help you become less tense.

You might find you prefer your sample at a different gauge depending on the properties of your yarn. Even with the same size stitches, a piece made from puffy, fluffy, or squishy yarn looks and feels very different from one made with smooth, incompressible, or tightly spun yarn. The most important thing to remember is to choose a hook size that's appropriate for the yarn and stitch pattern you're using and how tightly you crochet.

Swatching is the key to finding the perfect balance for your pattern and the look and feel you want to achieve. Once you find the best hook size for your yarn and stitch pattern, you can calculate the gauge from your swatch. If it's nowhere near what the pattern suggests but you love it anyway, you have several choices.

If your pattern is formed from a basic shape, like a rectangle, you can use the finished dimensions of the pattern and crochet more or fewer repeats than specified to create the same finished size piece. Or understand that your finished piece will differ in size from the pattern. So if the pattern calls for 4 stitches per inch and you're getting 6 stitches per inch (or whatever your unit of measure), your piece will end up being two-thirds the size.

Finally, for complex projects in which the finished size is important, if you don't like the drape of the crocheted fabric when you meet the gauge, your best bet is to choose a different yarn that's more suitable for the pattern and save the original yarn for another project.

Modifying Patterns

You don't always have to follow a pattern exactly. If you feel adventurous, you can experiment with modifying patterns to fit your purpose.

Change the color. Try to see past the colors used for a pattern sample. You can dramatically alter the look of a design by making it in colors that appeal to you (or your recipient if you're making a gift). Buy yarns in the colors that speak to you and you're already halfway to crocheting a piece you'll love.

Change the weight. Many crochet patterns work equally well at several scales. Working with a lighter yarn and a smaller hook gives you a delicate, fine result but might take a long time to complete. Working the same-sized project with a heavier yarn and a larger hook produces a bolder, thicker result—and in a fraction of the time.

Change the pattern. If you love the stitch pattern of an afghan but don't want to make something as large as a blanket, make it much narrower and you'll have an instant scarf. Or make a smaller version of a triangle shawl to form a head scarf or bandanna.

The same granny square pattern looks totally different when crocheted in a different color combination, using a finer weight of yarn, and with an appropriately smaller hook. The pattern for this granny square is on page 182.

How to Read a Pattern

Crochet patterns are written in shorthand so they take less space on the page. Stitch names are abbreviated and repeated sections are marked as such and only written out once.

Once you get used to the way patterns are written, they're far easier to read and follow without losing your place than if the entire pattern had been written out in full.

Rows and Rounds

Crochet patterns are worked in either rows or rounds. Each pattern row (or round) gives you the directions for working all the way across the top of your work (or all the way around your work). Rows and rounds are numbered as Row 1, Row 2, Row 3, etc., or Rnd 1, Rnd 2, Rnd 3, etc. At the end of each row/round, the number of stitches you should have made in that row/round is given in parentheses. This is a helpful checkpoint so you can see if you've made any mistakes before you move on.

Working into Specific Stitches

If a pattern says to work into *next st*, you work into the very next stitch. *sc in next st* means you work a single crochet into the next stitch. *2 hdc in next 4 sts* means you work 2 half double crochets into *each* of the next 4 stitches so you end up with a total of 8 hdcs. *(sc, ch 1, hdc) in next st* means all the stitches in the parentheses are worked into the same (next) stitch. In this case, you work a single crochet in the next stitch, chain 1, and work a half double crochet into the same stitch you worked the single crochet.

If a pattern says to work into a specific type of st— for example, *sc in next dc*—jump straight to the next dc stitch, ignoring all other stitches before you reach it.

If a pattern says to work into a *chain space (ch-sp)*, you work into the space underneath the loop formed by 1 or more chain stitches. To work this stitch, insert your hook into the space beneath the chain, not directly into any of the chain stitches.

Always read the introductory information at the start of a pattern before you begin crocheting. It contains essential information about the size(s) of the item, the type of yarn and hook you need, abbreviations used, and any special stitches called for in the pattern.

Repeats

Repeated instructions are indicated with parentheses (...), brackets [...], or asterisks * (or another symbol). For example, *(2 sc in next st, sc in next st) 4 times* means you repeat all the instructions within the parentheses 4 times. Work 2 single crochets in the next stitch and then 1 single crochet in the next stitch. Now go back to the beginning of the parentheses and repeat the same instructions into the following stitches: 2 sc in the next st followed by 1 sc in the next stitch. Go through the instructions twice more so you repeat the instructions a total of 4 times.

*2 sc in next st, sc in next st; rep from * 3 times means you repeat all the instructions from *** to *;* 3 times. Follow the instructions (2 single crochets in the next stitch and then 1 single crochet in the next stitch), and when you reach *rep from **, jump back to the asterisk and work the instructions again 3 more times. Note that after you crochet the first set of instructions, you repeat them 3 *more* times, so you'll end up working the instructions a total of 4 times.

An instruction can also be repeated all the way across a row (or around a round). For example, **dc in next st, ch 1, sk next st; rep from * across to last 2 sts, dc in last 2 sts* means you repeat the instruction (double crochet in the next stitch, chain 1, skip over the next stitch without working into it) over and over until you reach the specified point (the last 2 stitches of the row). Then you complete the row with a double crochet into each of the last 2 stitches.

Multiple Sizes

If a pattern includes multiple sizes, the information for the smallest size is given first, followed by the larger sizes in parentheses or brackets:

> Size: Small (Medium, Large)

> Ch 30 (36, 42)

This means you chain 30 stitches if you want to make a size small, 36 for medium, and 42 for large. Select the option at each point that corresponds to the size you're making.

Reading a Stitch Pattern

A *stitch pattern* is a set of instructions that tells you how to make a specific combination of crocheted stitches. Stitch patterns are usually given as a general formula so you can make a piece of any size and shape and they're based on repeats. The *stitch pattern repeat* tells you how many different stitches to make before you repeat the same instructions across the row and the *row repeat* tells you how many different rows to crochet before you repeat the same row instructions.

The *starting chain formula* tells you how many chains to start with so you don't end up with half a stitch pattern repeat at the end of your piece. The starting chain formula includes the stitch pattern repeat plus any additional chains you need to make at each edge and for the turning chain. For example, *ch a multiple of 10 sts plus 3* means you'll work any multiple of 10 chains (10, 20, 30, etc.) until the foundation is as long as you'd like the width of your piece to be. Then you'll crochet 3 more chains to complete the foundation chain.

All the tutorials and patterns in this book are written using U.S. terminology.

Terminology

Crochet stitches aren't named consistently worldwide, and even more confusingly, the same name is used to mean different stitches in different countries. Patterns published in the United Kingdom and countries with historically British influence use a different naming scheme from those published in North America.

Check where a pattern was published to get a good idea of which terminology is used. Also, there's no stitch called *single crochet* in U.K. terminology, so if you see *sc* anywhere, you know the pattern uses U.S. terminology. Here are the most common substitutions you'll need to convert a U.K. pattern to U.S. terminology and vice versa.

U.S. Name	U.K. Name
chain	chain
slip stitch	slip stitch
single crochet	double crochet
half double crochet	half treble crochet
double crochet	treble crochet
triple (or treble) crochet	double treble
back post double crochet	raised treble back
front post double crochet	raised treble front
gauge	tension
skip	miss
yarn over	yarn over hook

Crochet Abbreviations

To save space, stitch names are almost always abbreviated in crochet patterns, as are common repeated words. The following table shares some of the most common abbreviations you're likely to encounter in crochet patterns.

Not all abbreviations are completely standardized, so check your pattern's abbreviations list for any terms unfamiliar to you. This is typically located at the start of a pattern or they're all listed together at the front or back of a book.

Abbreviation	Meaning	Abbreviation	Meaning
BL	back loop	inc	increase
BP	back post	MC	main color
BPdc	back post double crochet	rep	repeat
BPtr	back post triple (treble) crochet	rnd(s)	round(s)
CC	contrast color	RS	right side
ch(s)	chain(s)	rsc	reverse single crochet
ch-sp(s)	chain space(s)	sc	single crochet
dc	double crochet	sc2tog	single crochet two together
dc2tog	double crochet two together	sk	skip
dec	decrease	sl st	slip stitch
fdc	foundation double crochet	sp(s)	space(s)
fhdc	foundation half double crochet	st(s)	stitch(es)
FL	front loop	t-ch	turning chain
FP	front post	tog	together
FPdc	front post double crochet	tr	triple (treble) crochet
FPtr	front post triple (treble) crochet	WS	wrong side
fsc	foundation single crochet	YO	yarn over
hdc	half double crochet		

Beyond the Basics

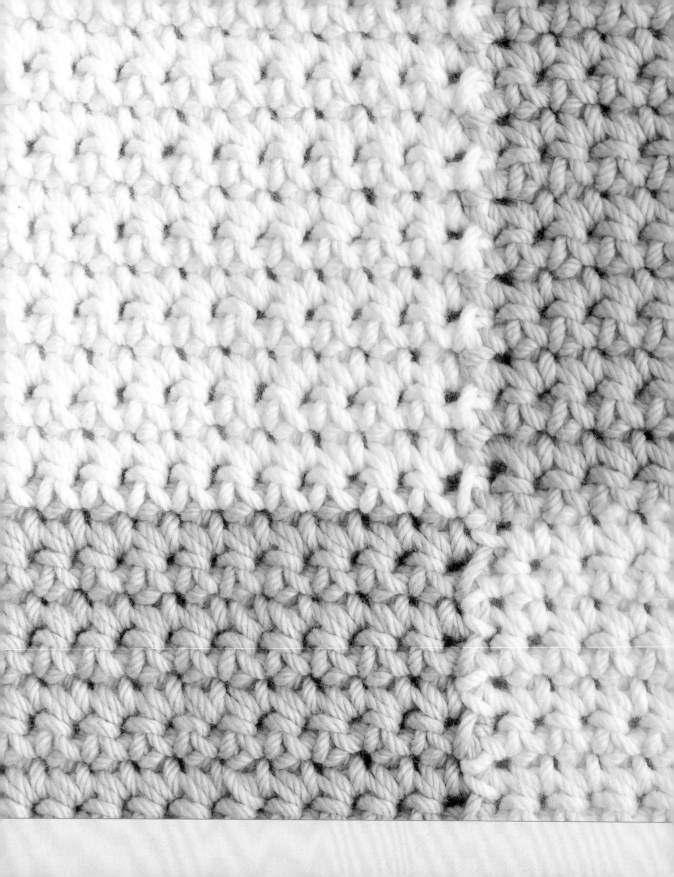

More Crochet Know-How

Joining New Yarn

Larger crochet projects, like blankets, shawls, and garments, usually require more than one ball of yarn. When you reach the end of one ball, you'll need to join a new ball to your project.

The easiest place to join new yarn is at the end of a row. If the item will be seamed or edged, you can hide the yarn ends in the seam or border. If you're running short of yarn and need to add the next ball, try to judge when to stop so you don't run out of yarn partway through a row. (I'm using a different color of yarn in these examples for clarity.) To join new yarn:

Begin the last stitch of the old yarn, but stop before you reach the final step (yarn over and draw through all the remaining loops on the hook).

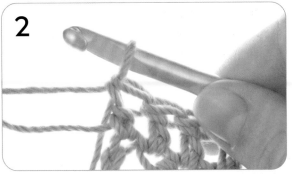

Leaving a 6-inch (15cm) starting tail on the new yarn, yarn over with the new yarn and draw it through the loops on your hook to complete the stitch.

weave these ends in later

Drop the old yarn, and continue crocheting with the new yarn. You can go back later and weave in both yarn ends.

Tying knots is unnecessary if you weave your ends in securely. If you find it difficult to switch to the new yarn and keep crocheting while the yarn ends are dangling free, tie the ends together in a simple knot until you've worked past them and then untie the knot before you weave in the ends.

Russian Join

An alternative way to join yarn at any point in the row without any waste is by using a Russian join. With this method, you splice the ends of the old and new balls together.

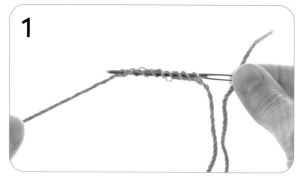

Thread the end of the working yarn through a yarn needle. Starting about 3 inches (7.5cm) down the working yarn, insert a yarn needle into the yarn strand by picking up some of the plies of the yarn with the needle and leaving others. (This is easier if you untwist the plies of the yarn a bit.)

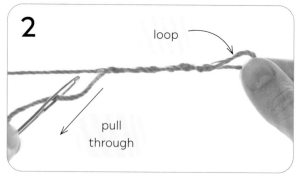

When you've worked the needle through about 2 inches (5cm) of yarn, carefully pull the needle and tail through the yarn strand so the yarn is woven back through itself, leaving a small loop. Remove the needle.

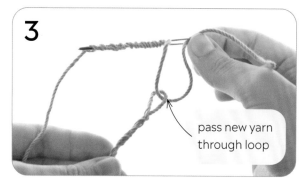

Thread the new yarn through the needle and pass it through the loop. Insert the needle into the new yarn strand, about 3 inches (7.5cm) down toward the ball of yarn, as you did for the first strand. Pull the needle through to weave the yarn back through itself, leaving you with another loop linked through the first.

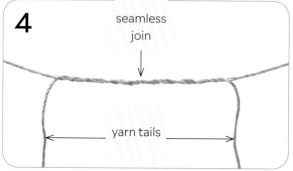

Pull each yarn tail in turn to shrink each loop. When both loops are closed, you have one joined strand of yarn, with each yarn end woven back into itself.

5

Trim the remainder of the dangling yarn tails.

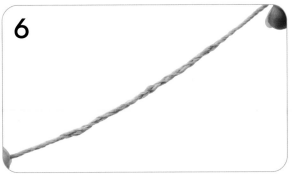

6

The joined yarn is ready for you to continue crocheting. The joined section will be slightly bulkier than the rest of the yarn but smooth and very strong.

To give the neatest finish, ignore the tails as you crochet with the joined yarn, letting them drop to the back of your work. Once the join is crocheted into your fabric, you can safely snip off the tails without weaving them in any further, as the yarn has already been woven into itself.

Changing Colors

Changing colors of yarn in a project can be confusing. The way crochet patterns are written, it's easy to think you should complete one stitch in the old color and then change color to begin the next stitch in the new color. But that's not actually the case. Doing it this way leaves a large dot of the old color visible within the new color. Instead, here's how to make a clean color change.

1

Begin the last stitch in the old color, but stop before you reach the final step (yarn over and draw through all the remaining loops on the hook).

2

Leaving a 6-inch (15cm) starting tail of the new color, yarn over with the new yarn.

3

The new color is now on the hook.

Draw the new yarn through the loops on your hook to complete the stitch with the new color.

4

Drop the old yarn to the back and continue crocheting with the new yarn. You can go back later and weave in both yarn ends.

When you need to change colors, watch for the approaching color change, and complete the last step of the stitch *before* the color change with the new color. This is such a universal rule, most patterns won't mention it.

Carrying Yarn

If you're switching between two or more colors, weaving in two ends every time you change color can be a lot of work. Instead, you can often *carry* the unused strand along until you need it again and then switch back without cutting the yarn. You can do this in one of several ways.

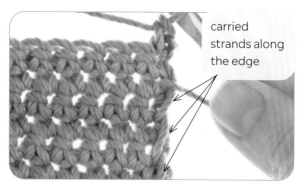

carried strands along the edge

crocheting over the carried yarn with each stitch

If you're working in stripes, you can leave the unworked yarn hanging at the end of the row after you change color. When you get back to that end, pick up the yarn and carry it loosely up along the edge of your work to the new row. After you finish, you could add a border to cover the carried yarn strands.

If you're swapping between two (or more) colors, you can lay the unused color across the top of the row and crochet over it to enclose the carried yarn inside your stitches until you need it again. Working over the carried yarn leaves both sides of the work looking tidy, so it's useful if you're making a reversible fabric.

Whenever you carry strands of yarn, the floating strands should lie flat along the surface of the fabric but be loose enough that they don't pull or pucker your fabric.

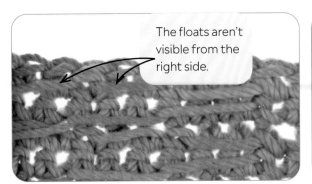

The floats aren't visible from the right side.

If the back of your work won't be seen, you can carry the unused color(s) loosely along the wrong side of your work. This is called *stranding* and it works best if the *floats* of yarn (the strands running along the back of the work) are only a few stitches long. If your floats are longer, you can either cut them and weave in the ends or work over the float every few stitches to prevent a long, loose loop of yarn from forming on the wrong side.

If you're only changing color occasionally or with a long span of one color, it's usually easiest to cut the yarn at every color change and weave in the ends. For the cleanest results, weave each yarn end into stitches of the same color.

Reading Charted Stitch Diagrams

A charted stitch diagram gives you a way to visualize a crochet pattern. The overall diagram looks similar to how your finished piece will look, with each stitch represented by a symbol.

Charts can complement—or in some cases even replace—a written pattern and are especially useful with lacy and motif-based patterns. They make it easier to understand where to insert your hook for the next stitch and you can see an overview of how the stitch pattern will come together before you even start crocheting.

Standard Stitch Symbols

The following table gives you the symbols for some commonly used stitches and techniques. These basic stitch symbols show the relationship of the stitches to each other: the double crochet symbol is twice as tall as the single crochet and the half double is midway in height between the two—just as with the real stitches. The taller stitches are crossed by short horizontal bars that represent the number of yarn overs you make to begin the stitch.

Symbol	Stitch
⬯	ch
● or •	sl st
✕ or ＋	sc
⊤	hdc
⊤	dc
⊤	tr
◯	magic ring

Variable Stitch Symbols

Combination stitches, such as shells, clusters, bobbles, puffs, popcorns, and picots, can be worked in different ways. The symbol is modified to reflect the specific components that form the stitch. The symbol shows which basic stitch to use and how many are combined to form the stitch.

Symbol	Stitch
	sc2tog decrease
	dc3tog cluster/decrease
	5-tr shell
	4-dc bobble
	3-hdc puff
	4-dc popcorn
	ch-3 picot (closed)
	ch-3 picot (open)

Modified Stitch Symbols

When you work a stitch into the front or back loop or around the front or back post of the stitch below, the stitch symbol is modified to reflect that. Post stitches use a hook at the bottom of the stitch to show that you work around the stitch below. Back- or front-loop-only stitches include a curved symbol below the stitch that represents the loop you work into. Foundation stitches show the stitch joined to the chain below. And for crossed stitches, the stitch that sits behind the other stitch is shown fainter than the stitch in front.

Symbol	Stitch
	FPdc
	BPdc
	sc in back loop only
	sc in front loop only
	foundation sc
	crossed dcs

When you start reading charts, try comparing the diagram with the written pattern and using one as a backup for the other. If something isn't clear to you in the chart, check it against the text, and vice versa. When you get the hang of reading stitch diagrams, you might not need to follow the text at all, although the written pattern will include additional details you'll need, such as the number of repeats to make and finishing instructions.

Reading a Chart

A charted stitch diagram shows the stitches of the crocheted fabric as seen from the right side. Each stitch is pictured above the stitch or space you should crochet it into.

If you're working in rows, start with the foundation at the bottom of the chart, move up to Row 1, and follow the stitches from right to left across the row. When you turn your work, move up to Row 2 and follow the stitches from left to right across the row (although you'll still be crocheting from right to left, as always).

If you're working in rounds, start from the central ring and follow the stitches counterclockwise around the ring. Keep following the stitches counterclockwise for every round unless the start of a round indicates with an arrow that you should change direction. In this case, turn your work and follow the stitches clockwise around the diagram (although you'll still be crocheting counterclockwise, as always).

The number at the start of each row corresponds to the row number in the written pattern. This helps you keep your place and shows you clearly where to go next. Alternating rows are usually shown in different colors to help you distinguish the stitches of one row from those of the next. Arrows are sometimes used to indicate start and end points or the direction you should follow on the chart.

Although a chart can show a whole small pattern, charts for larger pieces usually show a reduced sample that demonstrates how the repeating stitch pattern fits together. When you're crocheting the pattern, you'll duplicate the repeating section across the entire row.

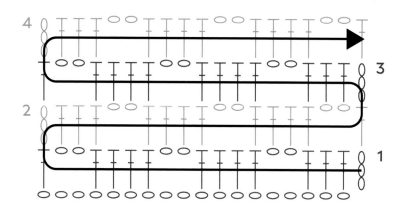

Colorblock
Potholder

With this fun project, you can practice your color changes and make a sturdy, heat-resistant potholder at the same time!

Although you change color with every row, you only need to cut the yarn once (halfway through the pattern), so you'll have minimal ends to weave in.

Basic Measurements

About 7 inches (17.5cm) square.

Yarn

About 60 yards (55m) worsted weight cotton in each of two colors. Shown in Knit Picks Dishie, 100% cotton.

Hook

U.S. I/9 (5.5mm)

Other Supplies

Yarn needle, scissors

New Techniques

Basic Edging (page 58)

How to Read a Pattern (page 76)

Changing Colors (page 90)

Notes

Every time you reach a color change, draw through the last loop of the stitch *before* the change with the new yarn color. Drop the old yarn to the back, but don't fasten off—you'll pick it up again in the next row.

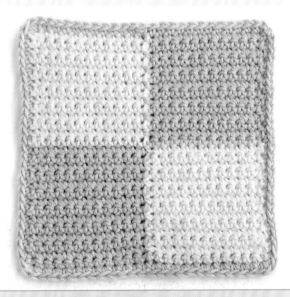

Colorblock Potholder

With the main color (MC), leave a 6-inch (15cm) starting tail and ch 25.

Row 1: sc in 2nd ch from hook, sc in next 11 chs. Change color, dropping MC yarn to the back and leaving a 6-inch (15cm) starting tail of the contrast color (CC). Sc in each remaining ch. (24 sts)

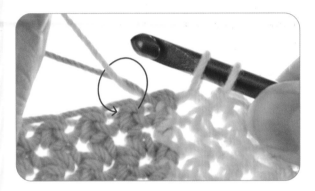

From Row 2 on, you'll pick up the yarn you dropped in the middle of the previous row. As you're about to complete the stitch before the color change with the new yarn, twist the two yarns together counterclockwise. This keeps both yarns in position without any loose loops so the join looks neat and tidy.

You'll notice your yarns tangle together more and more with each new row. Pause every few rows and pass one yarn ball around and around the other until the two strands are separate again and resume crocheting. It's much easier to do this than to keep going and be faced with a big tangle later!

Row 2: ch 1, turn, sc in next 12 sts. Change color. Sc in next 12 sts. (24 sts)

Repeat Row 2 12 times or until each color of your work forms a square block. Leaving a 6-inch (15cm) tail, cut the yarn you dropped in the middle of the last row. Draw through the final loop of the last stitch with the other color so you can begin crocheting with the alternate color.

Row 3: ch 1, turn, sc in next 12 sts. Leaving a 6-inch (15cm) starting tail, change color. Sc in next 12 sts. (24 sts)

Row 4: ch 1, turn, sc in next 12 sts. Change color. Sc in next 12 sts. (24 sts)

Repeat Row 4 12 times or as many times as you repeated Row 2.

Fasten off and cut both yarns, leaving a 6-inch (15cm) tail of each color.

Crochet a second square in the same way, but don't fasten off the MC yarn. Weave in the ends that hang from the centers of the squares. You also can weave in the ends that hang from the edges or just crochet over them as you work the edging to save time.

If you want to make a matching dishcloth or washcloth that doesn't need a double thickness for heat resistance, you can omit the second square and add the edging to the single square.

Place the first square on top of the second to begin the single crochet edging. You'll find it easier to crochet the squares together if you start with both the same way up so the stitches match along the edges. Insert your hook through the edges of both layers to begin each stitch, joining the squares as you crochet.

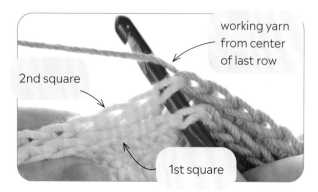

working yarn from center of last row

2nd square

1st square

Pick up the MC yarn from the center of the final row. Insert your hook under both loops of the next stitch (the first CC stitch) on both squares, draw up a loop, and ch 1.

Starting with the same stitch and crocheting through both layers with each stitch, sc in each stitch along the top and make 3 sc in the corner stitch. Sc into the end of each row down the side and make 3 sc in the next corner stitch. Repeat for the remaining sides, making 1 sc in each stitch or row edge and 3 sc in each corner. Sc in the remaining stitches along the top to complete the edging.

Join with sl st to first stitch (or use an invisible finish [page 124] for a smoother join).

Fasten off and weave in all remaining ends.

Increasing and Decreasing

Increasing

Increasing the number of stitches in a row or round is easy: To add a stitch, you simply work 2 stitches into the top of a stitch on the previous row.

Increasing is written as the number of stitches you'll make into that stitch, such as "2 dc in next st" or "3 sc in next st". Here's how to make a double crochet increase (2 dc in next st).

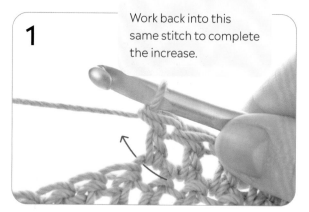

Work back into this same stitch to complete the increase.

Make a dc in the next stitch.

Make another dc in the same stitch.

Increasing at the Start of a Row

Increasing at the start of a row is a little different because the turning chain typically counts as the first stitch (unless you're working in single crochet). Here's how to increase at the start of a row in dc.

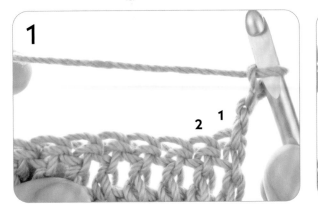

Ch 3 and turn your work. You usually skip the 1st stitch (at the base of the chain) and insert your hook into the 2nd stitch.

Instead, work the 1st dc into the 1st stitch at the base of the chain.

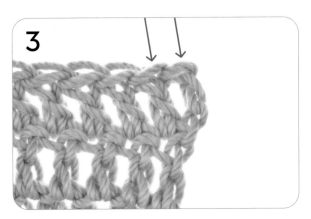

The turning chain plus this stitch count as 2 stitches, so you've added 1 stitch at the start of the row.

For multiple increases, unless you want to shape the fabric asymmetrically—for example, to create a toy or a fitted garment—it's best to space your increases evenly across the row (or around the round).

Decreasing

The simplest way to reduce the number of stitches in a row or round is by skipping a stitch, but this leaves a hole in your fabric. To keep your crochet looking more even, you can work decreases.

To create decreases, you work multiple stitches together, crocheting incomplete stitches and then completing all the stitches together at once at the top. The result is a triangular stitch that's wide at the bottom and narrow at the top. Decreases are named for the number and type of stitch being decreased (or *crocheted together*). For example, *sc2tog* means 2 single crochet stitches are combined into 1 and *dc3tog* means 3 double crochet stitches are combined into 1.

To work a decrease in any basic stitch, the pattern is the same: Make each stitch up to the final step and then complete all the stitches together. Let's see that in action.

Single Crochet 2 Stitches Together (sc2tog)

Insert your hook into the next stitch and draw up a loop.

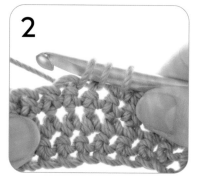

Instead of completing the sc, insert your hook into the next stitch and draw up a loop. (You now have 3 loops on the hook.)

Yarn over and draw through all 3 loops on the hook to complete the decrease.

Double Crochet 3 Stitches Together (dc3tog)

Yarn over, insert your hook into the next stitch, and draw up a loop. Yarn over and draw through 2 loops on the hook. (You now have 2 loops on the hook.)

Instead of completing the dc, yarn over, insert your hook into the next stitch, and draw up a loop. Yarn over and draw through 2 loops on the hook. (You now have 3 loops on the hook.)

Repeat step 2 once more, to make the third incomplete dc stitch. (You now have 4 loops on the hook.)

Yarn over, and draw through all 4 loops on the hook to complete the decrease.

The general rule for a decrease in any crochet stitch is to work each stitch of the decrease up to the final step (yarn over and draw through all the remaining loops on the hook) and then do the same for each of the other stitches in the decrease. You should end up with one more loop on your hook than the number of stitches being decreased. Yarn over and draw through all these loops to complete the decrease.

Practice Project 3:

Triangle Bunting

Crocheted bunting makes a perfect decoration— just choose an appropriate color scheme and you can use it for any occasion! Consider pastels for a baby shower, bright colors for a summer party, or seasonal colors for festivities.

Try both pattern triangle variants to practice increasing (bottom up) and decreasing (top down). They yield the same shape and size of flag, so you can mix and match the patterns.

Basic Measurements

Each flag is about 4½ inches (11.5cm) wide and tall.

Yarn

Small quantities of worsted weight yarn with any fiber content, in multiple colors. Each flag takes less than 15 yards (14m) of yarn. Shown in Knit Picks Shine Worsted, 60% cotton, 40% plant fiber.

Hook

U.S. I/9 (5.5mm)

Other Supplies

Yarn needle, scissors

New Techniques

Increasing (page 104)

Decreasing (page 106)

The border around each flag not only flattens out the bumps at the edges but also helps straighten out any curling, so your flags should hang flat without the need for blocking.

Top-Down Flag

Ch 16.

Row 1: sc in 2nd ch from hook and each remaining ch. (15 sts)

Row 2: ch 1, turn, sc2tog, sc in each remaining st across. (14 sts)

Rows 3 through 15: repeat Row 2. Your stitch count will decrease by 1 each row. (13 to 1 sts)

Don't turn your work or fasten off. Crochet a sc edging around each edge of the triangle, working 1 sc into the edge of each row, 1 sc along the top of each st, and (sc, hdc, sc) into each corner st. When you reach your starting yarn tail, crochet over it as you work the edging.

When you've crocheted all the way around the triangle, (sc, hdc, sc) in the final corner and then join with sl st to the next st. Fasten off and weave in the ends.

Bottom-Up Flag

Ch 2.

Row 1: 2 sc in 2nd ch from hook. (2 sts)

Row 2: ch 1, turn, 2 sc in next st, sc in each remaining st across. (3 sts)

Rows 3 through 14: repeat Row 2. Your stitch count will increase by 1 each row. (4 to 15 sts)

Row 15: ch 1, turn, sc in each st across.

Don't turn your work or fasten off. Crochet a sc edging around each side of the triangle as explained in the Top-Down Flag.

Bunting Assembly

Arrange the flags so they're all upright (the rows run horizontally across each flag) and right side up (the Vs around the edge of each flag are visible from the front). Then order them in a color arrangement you like. You'll be crocheting along the top of each flag to join them together into a garland. Use a contrasting color of yarn if desired.

Optional: To make a loop from which to hang the bunting, ch 10, sl st to 1st ch.

Sc in each st across the top of the 1st flag.

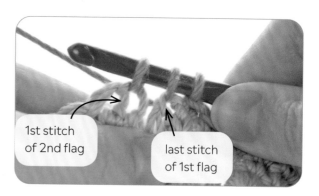

1st stitch of 2nd flag

last stitch of 1st flag

At the corner st, hold the 2nd flag next to the 1st and sc2tog across the last st of the 1st flag and the 1st st of the 2nd flag.

Sc across the top of each remaining flag, joining each to the next with a sc2tog across the last stitch of the old flag and the 1st stitch of the new flag.

Optional: To make a hanging loop on the other end, at the end of the final flag, ch 10, sl st to 1st ch.

Fasten off and weave in the ends. Hang your bunting with pride!

Crochet in the Round

Chain Start

To begin working in the round instead of a foundation chain, you'll work outward from a central point, increasing the number of stitches with each successive round.

Working into a Single Chain

The simplest way to do this is to work all the stitches of the first round into a single chain. You'll ch 1 plus the turning chain length for your stitch, so you'll ch 2 for single crochet or ch 4 for double crochet. Here's an example in single crochet.

Work all the stitches into this chain.

Ch 2.

Sc in the 2nd ch from the hook.

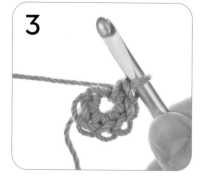

Make all the other stitches into the same chain.

To continue crocheting, you can either join the round before continuing or work in a spiral (page 118).

Working into a Chain Stitch Ring

Working into a single chain limits the number of stitches you can easily fit into it. A more versatile method is to form a circle from your chain stitches. With this technique, you can make the ring as large as you need it to be to leave a small or large hole in the center of the piece, as required. (This hole can be a decorative feature in some designs, but to avoid it, use a magic ring [page 116].)

To begin, make a short chain. Your pattern will give the exact length needed; in this example, crochet 5 chains.

Slip stitch into the farthest chain from the hook to join the chain into a ring.

To work the first round, insert your hook into the center of the ring, not into any of the individual chains that form the ring.

Chain the appropriate number of turning chains for the stitch you're making (see "Turning Chains" on page 48), then crochet all the stitches of the first round into the ring.

To continue crocheting, you can either join the round before continuing or work in a spiral (page 118).

Magic Ring

The magic ring, or *adjustable ring*, is commonly used when working in the round because it gives a very neat finish. Unlike the foundation chain ring method, no hole is left in the middle of your starting round when you use a magic ring.

You begin the magic ring just like a slipknot, but instead of tightening the loop into a knot, you crochet into it and then tighten it around your stitches. Here's how to make a single crochet magic ring.

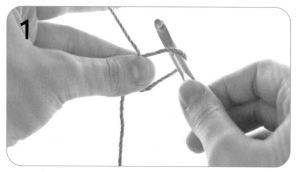

Make a loop a few inches from the end of your yarn. Grasp the join of the loop where the two strands overlap and insert your hook into the loop from front to back.

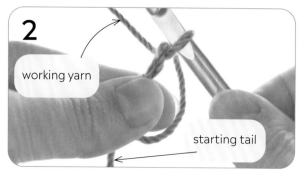

working yarn

starting tail

Draw up a loop, ensuring you yarn over with the working yarn, not the short starting tail.

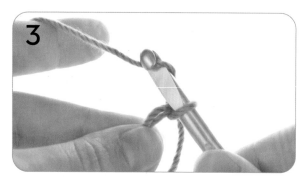

Yarn over, hooking the yarn from above the loop.

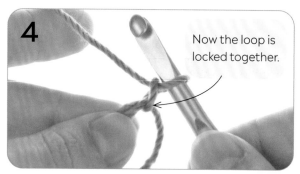

Now the loop is locked together.

Draw through the loop on the hook to form a ch 1. This ch doesn't count as a stitch.

5

Insert your hook into the loop so you're crocheting over the loop and the yarn tail.

6

Draw up a loop to begin your first sc and then complete the sc.

7

Work over the loop and the tail.

Continue to crochet over the loop and the tail until you've completed the required number of stitches for your first round.

8

Pull the starting tail to close the ring.

Holding your last stitch loosely between your right thumb and forefinger, pull the yarn tail with your left hand to draw the center of the ring tightly closed.

To continue crocheting, skip the ch 1 from the start of the round and work back into the first sc you made. You can either join the round before continuing or work in a spiral.

You can crochet into a magic ring with any crochet stitch. Just replace the ch 1 in step 4 with the appropriate length of chain for the stitch you're making. (See "Turning Chains" on page 48.) Note that as usual with stitches taller than sc, the turning chain counts as a stitch, so you'll work back into that chain at the end of the round.

Working in the Round

Once you've made your foundation for working in the round, you can either make each round as a separate ring, like a bull's-eye, or work in a spiral.

Working in a Continuous Spiral

Working in a spiral means you have no seam at the end of each round. This method works best for shorter stitches, such as single crochet, because there's a jog at the very end of the spiral. That jog is easier to disguise with a short stitch height.

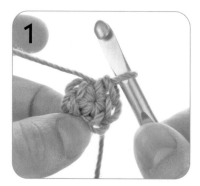

Crochet all the stitches of the first round into your starting ring.

To begin the second round, work the first stitch directly into the top of the first stitch of the first round.

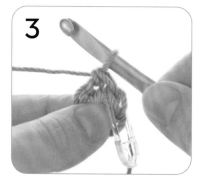

Mark the stitch you've just made with a stitch marker and continue with round 2 of your pattern.

Every stitch around the spiral looks the same, so there's no visual clue at the end of each round. By marking the first stitch of each round and moving the marker each time you begin a new round, you always know where the start of the round is. It's also a built-in safety check. If you overshoot the end of the round or finish too soon, you know there's a mistake somewhere in that round. You can find and fix it before you continue.

4

Work the last stitch of round 2 into the stitch before the marker.

5

Remove the marker and make the first stitch of round 3 into the previously marked stitch. Place the marker into the stitch you just made.

Continue to follow your pattern, moving up the marker as you begin each round. At the end of the spiral, smooth out the jog by slip stitching into the next stitch. If you're crocheting a spiral with taller stitches, smooth the jog with gradually shorter stitches before making the slip stitch.

A single crochet spiral with a slip stitch join.

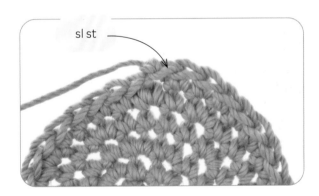

sl st

A double crochet spiral. At the end of your work, disguise the jog by adding extra stitches to gradually bring the hook down to the height of the next stitch: hdc, sc, and a sl st to join to the next stitch.

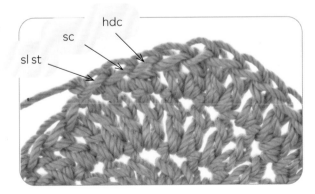

hdc

sc

sl st

Working in Joined Rounds

Joining your first and last stitches at the end of each round means you don't have that spiral jog at the end of your piece, but you do have a slight seam that runs along the line of your joins. Joined rounds are usually preferable for working in stitches taller than single crochet. The following examples are worked in double crochet.

Crochet all the stitches of the first round into your starting ring.

To complete the round, slip stitch into the first stitch of the round. This is the first stitch in sc or the top of the turning chain for taller stitches.

Now you've joined the round into a complete circle.

Chain to begin the next round.

You can turn your work at the end of each round or start the next round without turning. Each gives your work a different appearance because the fronts of all the stitches are visible on the right side if you don't turn and the backs of every other row are visible on the right side if you do turn. With the latter, the stitch pattern looks the same as when you crochet in rows.

If your pattern doesn't specify if you should turn between rounds, the default is to **not** turn.

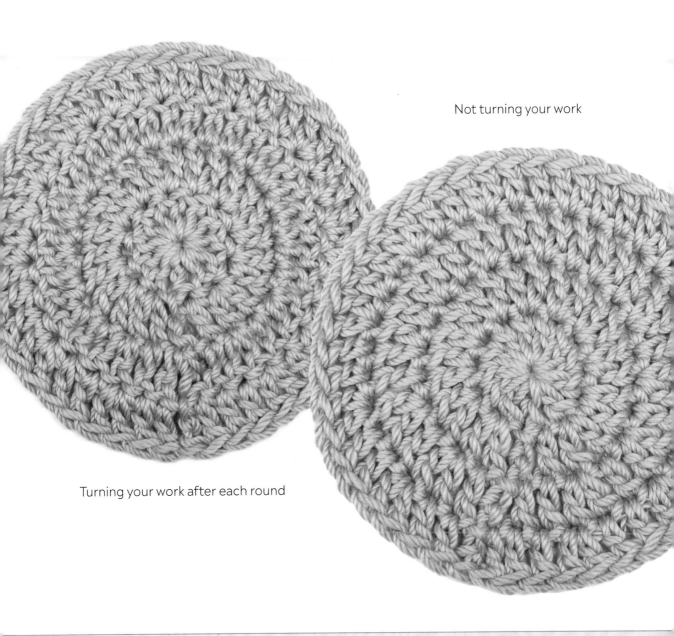

Not turning your work

Turning your work after each round

Standard Increases

When you're working in the round, you need to add stitches to each successive round as your piece grows larger. It's important you add the right number of stitches for the shape you want to create.

If you want a flat circle but add too many increases, the edges will start to ruffle. If you add too few increases, the piece will start to form a bowl shape. The height and width of each crochet stitch determines how many increases you need per round: The taller the stitch, the more increases you need per round to keep your crocheted circle flat.

Stitch	Stitches in First Round	Increases in Subsequent Rounds
sc	6	6
hdc	8	8
dc	12	12
tr	18	18

For each stitch except the single crochet, if you're working in joined rounds, the turning chain counts as the first stitch of the following round. For example, the 12 stitches that make up Rnd 1 in dc are formed from the turning chain plus 11 more dc stitches.

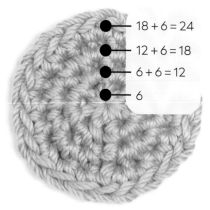

18 + 6 = 24
12 + 6 = 18
6 + 6 = 12
6

Single crochet is worked in multiples of 6.

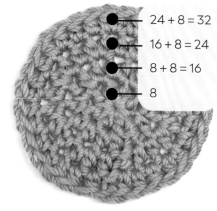

24 + 8 = 32
16 + 8 = 24
8 + 8 = 16
8

Half double crochet is worked in multiples of 8.

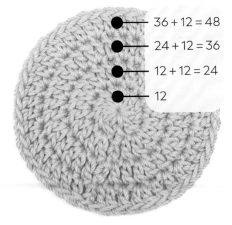

36 + 12 = 48
24 + 12 = 36
12 + 12 = 24
12

Double crochet is worked in multiples of 12.

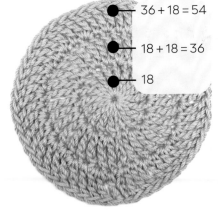

36 + 18 = 54
18 + 18 = 36
18

Triple (treble) crochet is worked in multiples of 18.

If you start with the correct number of stitches from the table on the previous page for Rnd 1, you'll increase in every stitch for Rnd 2, in every other stitch for Rnd 3, in every third stitch for Rnd 4, etc. If you stack the increases on top of each other in each round, your piece will start to develop straight sides with a corner at each increase point. For example, a single crocheted circle becomes hexagonal as it grows larger. To prevent this, you can stagger the positions of the increases in each round, keeping them equally spaced around the circle.

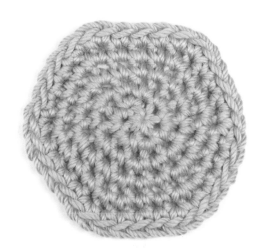

With stacked increases, a single crochet circle starts to look hexagonal.

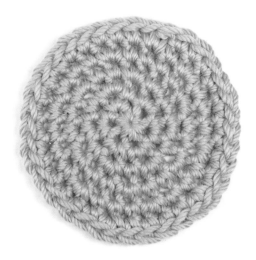

Staggering the increases will help keep the circle circular.

Invisible Finish

The invisible finish is the best way to fasten off when you're working in the round because it leaves an undisturbed ring of sideways Vs around the edge of the piece. With this technique, you use a needle to stitch a duplicate of the V at the top of the first stitch of the round.

1

At the end of the final round, don't join the last stitch to the first stitch of the round. Cut the yarn, leaving a 6-inch (15cm) tail.

2

Pull on the remaining loop on the hook, increasing its size until the tail pulls through to the top.

3

You'll duplicate these loops to make the join.

Thread the tail through a yarn needle.

4

Skip the first stitch and insert the needle from front to back under both loops of the second stitch.

5

Pull the yarn through, but don't draw the stitch tight.

6

Insert the needle back into the middle of the final stitch, between the 2 loops, and pass under the stitch's back vertical bar.

7

The new loop you formed covers the V of the first stitch of the round.

8

Here's the join.

Pull the yarn tail gently until the loop is the same size as the V at the top of all your other stitches and weave in the remaining tail. (See "Weaving in Ends" on page 60). The finished join should be practically indistinguishable from your other stitches!

Practice Project 4:

Circular Coasters

Practice working in the round while making something decorative and useful. A set of these coasters makes a great gift and you can make an entire set from one ball of yarn.

Basic Measurements

About 3.75 inches (9.5cm) diameter.

Yarn

About 12 yards (11m) worsted weight cotton or cotton blend yarn per coaster. Shown in Knit Picks Dishie, 100% cotton.

Hook

U.S. I/9 (5.5mm)

Other Supplies

Yarn needle, scissors

New Techniques

Magic Ring (page 116)

Working in the Round (page 118)

Make a magic ring.

Rnd 1: ch 2 (counts as hdc, here and throughout), 7 hdc in ring. Join with sl st to top of ch 2. (8 sts)

Pull the ring tightly closed.

Rnd 2: ch 2, hdc in same st, 2 hdc in next 7 sts. Join with sl st to top of ch 2. (16 sts)

Rnd 3: ch 1 (doesn't count as a st, here and throughout), sc in same st, (ch 1, sc in next st) 15 times, ch 1. Join with sl st to 1st st. (32 sts, including chs)

Rnd 4: ch 2, 3 hdc in next 15 ch1-sps, 2 hdc in next ch1-sp. Join with sl st to top of ch 2. (48 sts)

Rnd 5: ch 1, sc in same st, (ch 1, sk next st, sc in next st) 23 times, ch 1, sk next st, join with sl st to 1st st. (48 sts, including chs)

Fasten off and weave in the ends.

Finishing Techniques

Blocking

Blocking is the process of using moisture to relax the yarn's fibers and set stitches. Blocking can help straighten edges and coax pieces into the desired size and shape, which is especially important for garments and pieces that will be joined together.

Not all crochet needs to be blocked into shape, but blocking also helps smooth and straighten your stitches as well as even out any minor variances in your tension while you were crocheting.

You can block your work in several ways: *spray blocking* is the simplest, *steam blocking* gives the fastest result, and *wet blocking* is the most thorough. For every method, you need a flat surface to place your work on and pin into. You can either lay a thick towel over a flat padded surface (such as your ironing board, a carpeted floor, or even your bed) or buy a set of connectable foam mats.

Pinning Your Pieces

Whichever blocking method you choose, you usually need to pin your pieces into shape before leaving them to dry. Always use rustproof pins to prevent rust stains from ruining your work. For motifs or other pieces you'll be joining together, be sure to pin each piece to the same size so the edges match. If you're making a garment or item with specific dimensions, use the schematic from the pattern to pin each piece to the correct dimensions.

Lay out each piece with the right side up. Smooth it roughly into shape, working from the center out. Start pinning at the corners, easing the piece into shape as you go and using a measuring tape to ensure your piece is square and even. Add a pin halfway along the edge, using the measuring tape to verify you're pinning straight. Keep adding pins halfway between the previous pins until the fabric edge is straight and even.

Spray Blocking

Spray blocking is easy and fast: All you need is a spray bottle filled with water. Lay your piece on your blocking surface and smooth or pin it into position. Spray the piece evenly with water until the surface is saturated. Gently pat the surface to help the moisture penetrate into the yarn fibers. Leave your work undisturbed until thoroughly dry. This could take up to 24 hours depending on the temperature in your room and how thoroughly you saturated the yarn.

Steam Blocking

Steam blocking uses the heat and moisture of steam to relax and set the stitches. You can steam block using your household steam iron (and if it has a "shot of steam" feature, this process will be much faster!) or a handheld clothes steamer.

You can steam block almost any yarn, provided you're careful to keep the iron hovering above the surface of your crochet without touching it. Acrylic and other man-made fibers will melt if they come into direct contact with a hot iron. Also, don't use plastic-headed pins when steam blocking. The plastic will melt if your iron accidentally makes contact with them.

Lay your piece on your blocking surface and smooth or pin it into position. Hold the iron or steamer about 1 inch (2.5cm) above the surface of your crochet. **Don't** *let it come into contact with the yarn.* Steam until the entire surface is

damp and gently pat the surface to help the moisture penetrate into the yarn fibers. Leave your work undisturbed until thoroughly dry. This could take up to 24 hours depending on the temperature in your room and how thoroughly you saturated the yarn.

Wet Blocking

Wet blocking involves complete immersion of your piece in water before you coax it into shape. Thoroughly saturating the stitches enables you to completely reshape your piece.

Fill your sink with lukewarm water. You can also add some no-rinse wool wash if you want. Immerse your piece in the water and push down gently until the entire piece is saturated. Leave the piece to soak for about 20 minutes.

While supporting the entire piece so it doesn't stretch under its own weight, lift it from the water and gently squeeze without wringing. Continue squeezing to press out as much water as you can.

Lay out the piece on a clean towel. Roll up the towel and squeeze the rolled towel to remove as much of the remaining moisture from the piece as possible.

Lay the damp piece on your blocking surface, smooth it into position, and pin it to keep it in shape if needed.

Leave your work undisturbed until thoroughly dry. This could take 24 hours or longer depending on the temperature in your room, the thickness of the yarn, and how much moisture is left when you begin blocking.

Blocking Lace

Crocheted lace is almost magically transformed by the blocking process. As you stretch open the stitches, you reveal the detail of the stitch pattern and turn your crochet from a crumpled mass into a beautiful flowing fabric.

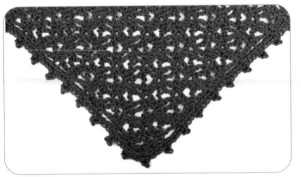

Before blocking

After blocking

To block crocheted lace, you use the wet blocking method. But after soaking and removing excess moisture, you also stretch the lace to open the stitch pattern. (Although it's not essential, if you plan to crochet many lacy items, it's worth investing in stainless-steel *blocking wires*, which help you block perfectly straight edges with minimal pinning.)

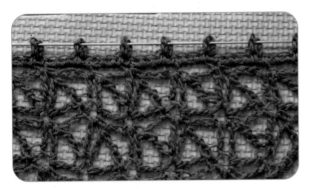

The edge will curve if you don't use enough pins.

To make it easier to block, weave a blocking wire along the entire straight edge of your work, passing it through every stitch or row edge or each tip of a pointed edging. To hold the piece in place, add a few pins to keep the wire in position.

If you don't have blocking wires, insert a pin into *every* stitch, row edge, or point to achieve the same effect. Using too few pins leaves the piece less stretched between the pins, so the edges won't be straight.

Joining

When joining crocheted pieces together, you usually use the same yarn you used to crochet the pieces so the seam will blend in. You can either crochet the pieces together or sew them using a yarn needle.

Joining motifs is straightforward because you should have the same number of stitches along each edge, which makes it easy to either sew or crochet the pieces together, stitch by stitch. Seaming pieces worked in rows (for example, to make a garment or a bag) is more challenging because you have to work into the row edges. The number of stitches might not match, and for taller rows, you might need to make more than one joining stitch per row.

Whichever joining method you use, it's best to block your crocheted pieces before you start to straighten the edges and ensure the pieces are exactly the same size.

I'm using a different color of yarn in these examples for clarity.

To join large pieces or if you have a different number of stitches on each of your starting pieces, use locking stitch markers to hold the pieces together along the seam line while you join them. Insert a stitch marker through the edge of both pieces at both ends of the seam line and keep adding more markers halfway between the previous ones until the pieces are linked every 2 inches (5cm) or so. Your pieces will remain matched all the way along their length as you seam.

Whip Stitch

The simplest sewn join is a whip stitch (also called an *overcast stitch*) seam. It's fast and easy, but the stitches are visible from both sides, so you'll get the neatest result if you're joining two pieces of the same color with a new length of the same color of yarn.

Hold the two pieces with the wrong sides together and pass your yarn needle from front to back under both loops of the first stitch on each piece.

Bring the needle back to the front and insert it under both loops of the next stitch on each piece. Draw the yarn taut to the fabric.

Repeat for each pair of stitches along the edge of the work.

The finished seam lies flat with a line of visible stitches on both sides.

Mattress Stitch

Also known as a *ladder stitch,* a mattress stitch forms bars running between the two pieces like the rungs of a ladder. When you pull the yarn tight, the bars disappear, leaving an almost invisible join. Mattress stitch is always worked from the right side, so you can check how neat your stitches look as you work.

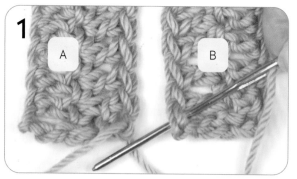

Lay your pieces (A and B) side by side, with the right sides facing up. Leaving a 6-inch (15cm) yarn tail, insert your needle down through the first edge stitch of A and then down through the first edge stitch of B.

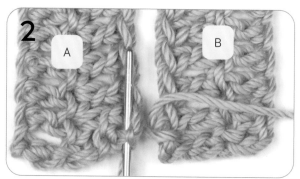

Now insert your needle back down through the first stitch of A and up through the second stitch of A.

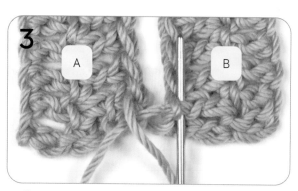

Cross over to B and insert your needle back down through the first stitch and up through the second.

Repeat for the next few stitches, inserting your needle back down through the previous stitch on that side and up through the next and then crossing back to the other side. You'll form horizontal bars of yarn between each piece.

5

Pull the yarn taut to draw the pieces together but not so tightly that the seam puckers.

6

Continue along the seam, pulling the yarn to draw the bars closed every few stitches.

7

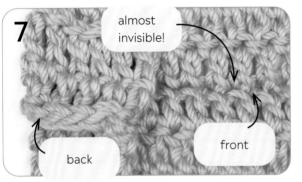

almost invisible!

back

front

If worked in the same color yarn, the finished seam is invisible from the front. The seamed stitches roll to the back, making a slight ridge.

With all sewn seams, take special care to secure your yarn well at each end of the seam. Unlike crocheted stitches, sewn stitches aren't locked together and the entire seam can unravel if one end of the yarn comes free.

Slip Stitch or Single Crochet Seam

Crocheting your pieces together is faster and easier than sewing, especially when joining motifs together. Hold or pin your pieces with the wrong sides together to make a seam with a ridge or with the right sides together to hide the ridge on the back of your work.

Slip stitch (or single crochet) through the first stitch of both pieces, inserting your hook through both loops on each piece to begin the stitch.

Repeat for each pair of stitches along the edge of the work.

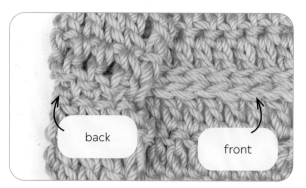

A slip stitch seam is ridged on the side you work it and almost invisible on the other side. (Slip stitches have no stretch, so keep your stitches loose and even to avoid puckering your fabric.)

A single crochet seam gives a more pronounced decorative ridge on the front and a slightly stretchier seam.

You can also create these seams by crocheting through the back loop only on each piece. This gives a slightly flatter but less sturdy join.

Flat Slip-Stitched Seam

This method is slower, but it creates a beautifully flat, symmetrical result for joining motifs. Lay your pieces side by side, with the right sides facing up. You'll be working into the back loops only of each stitch along the edges. These are the loops that lie closest together along the outer edge of each piece.

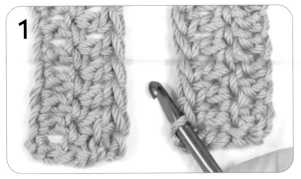

To begin each slip stitch, insert your hook from top to bottom through the back loop of the first stitch on the right piece.

Insert your hook from top to bottom through the back loop of the first stitch on the left piece, then yarn over and draw through all the loops on the hook.

Repeat for each stitch along the edge, inserting your hook from top to bottom through the back loop of both stitches before completing the sl st. Keep your slip stitches loose and even so they don't pucker your fabric.

back

front

The result is a flat row of chains that lie between each piece on the front and a line of stitches on the back.

Caring for Your Work

After all the work that goes into completing a beautiful crocheted item, you'll want it to last, so caring for it properly is important.

The best way to care for your crocheted pieces is to follow the care instructions from the yarn's ball band. This should help keep your work looking good for years to come.

It's also a good idea to keep a record of your crochet projects. A book or folder with a page or pocket for each project lets you easily find the information you need. You can keep a ball band, preferably with a scrap of the yarn tied around it, with the record of your project so you can look up how to care for your yarn if you forget.

Washing

If you no longer have the yarn's care instructions, it's best to err on the side of caution and hand wash and hand dry your crocheted pieces. When hand washing, use a mild detergent or a dedicated wool wash designed for hand washing garments.

Don't wring out your work—this stretches your stitches. Instead, roll up your crochet pieces in towels and press out as much moisture as possible before drying.

If you're giving your crocheted item as a gift, be sure to include a card or tag with the care information so your recipient knows how to look after it. Include all the washing information from the yarn's ball band and any additional instructions specific to your piece, such as whether it needs to be laid flat to dry and/or blocked into shape.

Drying

Whenever possible, dry your crocheted work flat because hanging it to dry can cause it to stretch out of shape. Some fibers are very heavy when wet and the weight of the piece itself can cause it to stretch vertically.

You might need to reblock your work after washing or at least lay the piece flat and tweak it into shape before letting it dry.

Ironing

Don't iron crocheted work unless a pattern specifically calls for it. At best, the pressing will squash your stitches and flatten the texture. Some yarns, particularly man-made fibers, might be damaged by the heat.

Easy Stitch Gallery

Easy Stitch
Patterns

The beauty of crochet is you can create a huge variety of stitch patterns from a few simple stitches. For example, you can make all the patterns in this chapter with only the most basic stitches: chain, single crochet, half double crochet, and double crochet. What's more, you can use these stitch patterns to make any rectangular-shaped object, such as a dishcloth, scarf, or blanket.

To begin each pattern, use the starting chain formula to crochet a chain of the desired width of your item. Then continue crocheting until the piece is as long as you want it. To get started, use the starting chain formula. (See "Reading a Stitch Pattern" on page 78.)

Single Crochet Ribbing

Crocheting in back loops (BL) only leaves a horizontal ridge at the base of each stitch, which works up into a stretchy textured ribbing.

Ch any number of sts.

Row 1: sc in 2nd ch from hook and in each remaining ch across.

Row 2: ch 1, turn, sc in BL of each st across.

Repeat Row 2 for the pattern.

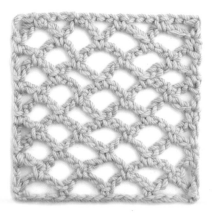

Granite Stitch

This simple stitch has many names. It's also known as *moss stitch* and *seed stitch*.

Ch an even number of sts.

Row 1: sc in 2nd ch from hook and in each remaining ch across.

Row 2: ch 1, turn, *sc in next st, ch 1, sk next st; rep from * across to last st, sc in last st.

Row 3: ch 1, turn, sc in next st, *sc in next ch1-sp, ch 1, sk next st; rep from * across to last 2 sts, sc in next ch1-sp, sc in last st.

Row 4: ch 1, turn, sc in next st, *ch 1, sk next st, sc in next ch1-sp; rep from * across to last 2 sts, ch 1, sk next st, sc in last st.

Repeat Rows 3 and 4 for the pattern.

Chain Mesh

With a simple pattern of chains and single crochets, you can create a lacy trellis of stitches. With very open patterns like this, blocking is an important step to open the mesh.

Ch a multiple of 4 sts plus 2.

Row 1: sc in 2nd ch from hook, *ch 5, sk next 3 ch, sc in next ch; rep from * across.

Row 2: ch 5 (counts as dc + ch 2), turn, *sc in next ch5-sp, ch 5; rep from * across to last ch5-sp, sc in last ch5-sp, ch 2, dc in last st.

Row 3: ch 1, turn, sc in next st, ch 5, *sc in next ch5-sp, ch 5; rep from * across to end, sc in 3rd ch of t-ch.

Repeat Rows 2 and 3 for the pattern.

To make a straight edge along the top of your piece, end with a Row 3 and continue to Row 4:

Row 4 (optional): ch 4 (counts as hdc + ch 2), turn, *sc in next ch 5-sp, ch 3; rep from * across to last ch5-sp, sc in last ch5-sp, ch 2, hdc in last st.

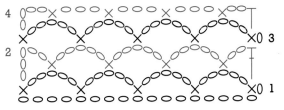

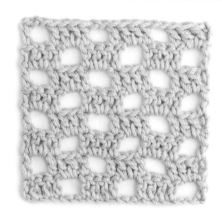

Up-and-Down Stitch

A pretty combination of short and tall stitches makes a solid, lightly textured fabric.

Ch a multiple of 2 sts plus 1.

Row 1: sc in 2nd ch from hook, *dc in next ch, sc in next ch; rep from * across to last ch, dc in last ch.

Row 2: ch 1, turn, *sc in next dc, dc in next sc; rep from * across to end.

Repeat Row 2 for the pattern.

Filet Squares

Filet crochet designs are made by alternating empty and filled blocks of stitches. By swapping the ch 2 and 2 dc stitches that form the middle of each block, you can vary the design.

Ch a multiple of 6 sts plus 3.

Row 1: dc in 4th ch from hook (unworked chs count as dc), dc in next 2 chs, ch 2, sk next 2 chs, *dc in next 4 chs, ch 2, sk next 2 chs; rep from * across to last ch, dc in last ch.

Row 2: ch 3 (counts as dc), turn, 2 dc in next ch2-sp, dc in next st, ch 2, sk next 2 sts, *dc in next st, 2 dc in next ch2-sp, dc in next st, ch 2, sk next 2 sts; rep from * across to last st, dc in top of t-ch.

Repeat Row 2 for the pattern.

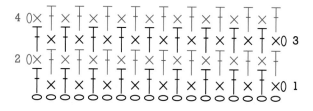

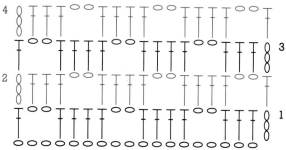

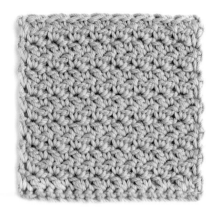

Ripple

The stacked increases and decreases in this pattern turn a line of straight stitches into graceful rippling waves—great for scarves and blankets.

Ch a multiple of 12 sts plus 3.

Row 1: dc in 4th ch from hook (unworked chs count as dc), dc in next 3 chs, dc2tog twice, *dc in next 3 chs, 2 dc in next 2 chs, dc in next 3 chs, dc2tog twice; rep from * across to last 4 chs, dc in next 3 chs, 2 dc in last ch.

Row 2: ch 3 (counts as dc), turn, dc in same st, dc in next 3 sts, dc2tog twice, *dc in next 3 sts, 2 dc in next 2 sts, dc in next 3 sts, dc2tog twice; rep from * across to last 4 sts, dc in next 3 sts, 2 dc in top of t-ch.

Repeat Row 2 for the pattern.

Grit Stitch

The stitches in this pattern slant in alternate directions with each row, giving a light diagonal texture.

Ch a multiple of 2 sts plus 1.

Row 1: sc in 2nd ch from hook and in each remaining ch across.

Row 2: ch 2, turn, sk first st, *(sc, dc) in next st, sk next st; rep from * across to last st, sc in last st.

Row 3: ch 2, turn, (sc, dc) in each dc across, sc in top of t-ch.

Repeat Row 3 for the pattern.

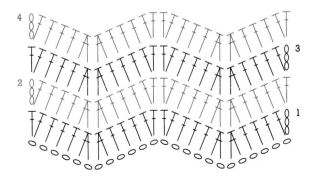

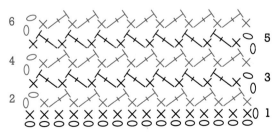

PART 3

Taking It Further

CHAPTER 11

Decorative Stitches

Shells, Fans, and V Stitches

Shells, fans, and V stitches make lovely edgings on crocheted pieces. The process of creating these three decorative stitches is similar.

The terms *shell* and *fan* are sometimes used interchangeably, but typically, a shell is formed from a solid group of stitches, while the stitches in a fan are separated by chains so they look like spokes. A *V stitch* is a special case with only two stitches separated by one or more chains, which makes the overall stitch look like a V. Each stitch has one or more skipped stitches before and after it to allow space for the width of the shell.

Infinite varieties of these stitches exist. Here are some examples, worked into a row of double crochet. (When these stitches are called for in a pattern, it will give the details for the specific shell, fan, or V stitch used.)

 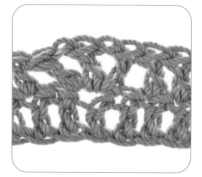 

Shell stitch: skip the next stitch and make 5 dc into the following stitch.

Fan stitch: skip the next stitch and make (dc, ch 1, dc, ch 1, dc) into the following stitch.

V stitch: skip the next stitch and make (dc, ch 1, dc) into the following stitch.

To continue with the pattern for each of these, skip the next stitch and dc in the following stitch.

Surrounding these stitches with shorter stitches gives the shell or fan space to form a more spread out, scalloped shape.

This solid shell is framed by sc stitches before and after. To make it, skip the next 2 stitches and make 5 dc into the next stitch.

Skip the next 2 stitches to complete the shell. To continue with the pattern, sc into the next st.

This fan takes up the same space as the previous shell, but it has a more open look. Instead of making 5 dc into the base stitch, make (dc, ch 1, dc, ch 1, dc) into the stitch.

Crossed Stitches

Crossed stitches give your crochet a more advanced look, but this method of stitching is actually quite simple.

To cross a pair of tall stitches, you skip a stitch, complete a stitch, and work the next stitch into the skipped stitch so the two create an X shape. You can cross stitches in three ways: You can work the second stitch behind, in front of, or wrapped around the first stitch. If a pattern doesn't specify which way to cross the stitches, working *behind* the first stitch is much easier than working in front.

All crossed stitches begin with the same first stitch: Skip a stitch and crochet into the following stitch. (I used double crochet stitches for these examples.)

Cross Behind

To make the crossed stitch, work into the skipped stitch.

Tilt your work forward or fold the first stitch forward so you can see the skipped stitch from behind the first stitch.

Yarn over, insert your hook into the skipped stitch, and complete the dc as usual. The second stitch crosses behind the first.

The wrapped cross works best with double crochet stitches because the cross happens near the base of the stitches and can look unbalanced with taller stitches.

Cross in Front

1 To make the crossed stitch, work into the skipped stitch.

2 Tilt your work forward and fold the first stitch backward so you have access to the skipped stitch from the front.

3 This maneuver is a bit tricky.

Keeping the yarn in front of the first stitch, yarn over, insert your hook into the skipped stitch, and complete the dc as usual. The second stitch crosses in front of the first.

Wrapped Cross

1 Yarn over and insert your hook into the skipped stitch, working in front of the first stitch.

2 With the yarn at the back, yarn over and draw up a loop, bringing the loop around the first stitch.

3 Complete the dc as usual. The second stitch encloses the base of the first.

Post Stitches

Post stitches are formed by crocheting around the post, or main stem, of the stitch below. This adds texture by bringing the stitch in front of or behind the stitch below. Post stitches can be combined to form textural patterns, such as ribs and cables.

You can work post stitches around the post of any stitch, but they're most often worked around dc or taller stitches because the larger spaces between these taller stitches make it easier to insert your hook around the post.

Front Post Double Crochet (FPdc)

To form a front post stitch, you work around the post of the stitch below, inserting your hook from the front, behind the post of the stitch, and back out to the front.

1. Yarn over and insert your hook from front to back to front around the post of the stitch below.

2. Yarn over and draw up a loop by bringing the hook back around the post of the stitch.

3. Complete the stitch as a double crochet stitch: (Yarn over and draw through 2 loops twice.)

Back Post Double Crochet (BPdc)

To form a back post stitch, you work around the post of the stitch below, inserting your hook from the back, in front of the post of the stitch, and back out to the back.

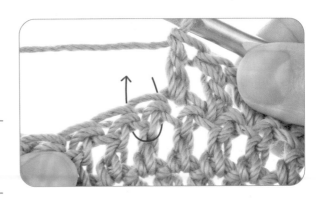

Post stitches are also known as *raised stitches* and *relief stitches*.

Yarn over and insert your hook from back to front to back around the post of the stitch below. (You might find this easier to do if you tilt your work forward first so you have better access to the back of the piece.)

Yarn over and draw up a loop by bringing the hook back around the post of the stitch.

Complete the stitch as a double crochet stitch: (Yarn over and draw through 2 loops twice.)

Spike Stitches

Spike stitches are worked around existing stitches to extend down to one (or more) rows below. The resulting spike of yarn is visible on both sides of the finished fabric, giving your work a nice design.

You can use a single color of yarn when making spikes to add texture, but they have the most visual impact when the row with the spikes is a different color from the base row(s) the spikes extend down into.

You can form a spike stitch extending into any space below the next stitch.

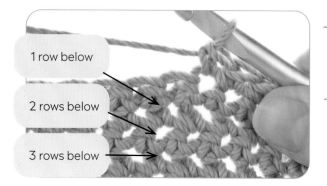

1 row below

2 rows below

3 rows below

Spike stitches are also known as *long stitches* and *dropped stitches*.

1 Insert your hook into the space below the next stitch. Here we're using the space 1 row below.

2 Yarn over and draw up a loop until it reaches the height of your previous stitch so your hook is horizontal.

3 Complete the stitch as a single crochet: Yarn over and draw through both loops on the hook.

Be careful not to pull the extended loops that form the spikes too tightly. The spikes should lay flat against the surface of the underlying fabric without distorting it.

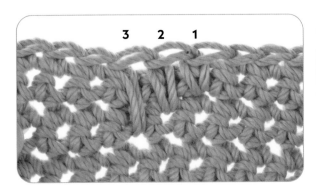

These spike stitches are worked into stitches 1 row, 2 rows, and 3 rows below.

These spikes are worked with different lengths in contrasting colors. The pictured pattern is worked as follows: *spike st into st 1 row below, sc in next st, spike st into st 2 rows below, sc in next st; rep from * across to end.

Chainless Foundations

Instead of making a foundation chain and then your first row of stitches, you can combine the two and create the chain and first row in a single step. Unlike a chain, chainless foundation stitches create a stretchy, elastic edge.

You'll be crocheting two rows at once, so it takes a bit longer to work a chainless foundation than a chain, but it's worth the time. It's much easier to work back into a chainless foundation than to work into a chain and you won't have to worry about the chain getting twisted or being overly tight.

You can use this technique to replace the first row of any pattern. Simply ignore the chain and replace the first row with the equivalent number of chainless foundation stitches. Note that chainless foundation stitches form vertically, so the tops of your stitches are on the right of your work and the bottom chains are on the left.

Foundation Single Crochet (fsc)

1

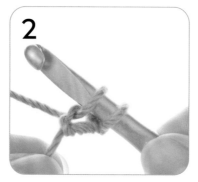

2

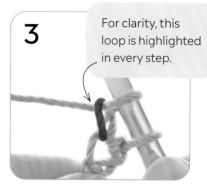

3

For clarity, this loop is highlighted in every step.

To make the first fsc stitch, ch 2. You'll be working into the 2nd chain from the hook.

Insert your hook into the 2nd chain from the hook and draw up a loop.

Yarn over and draw through 1 loop on the hook. This forms the chain you'll work into with your next stitch.

4

Yarn over and draw through 2 loops on the hook. This forms the single crochet. You now have 1 fsc complete.

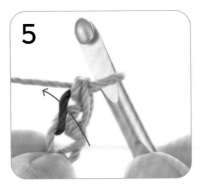

5

Work each subsequent fsc stitch by inserting the hook under the 2 loops that form the chain at the bottom of the previous stitch.

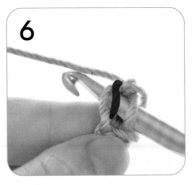

6

Insert the hook under the top and back loops of the chain.

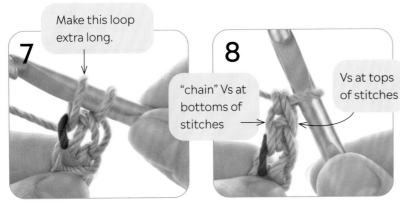

Make this loop extra long.

7

"chain" Vs at bottoms of stitches

Vs at tops of stitches

8

Draw up a loop until your hook is horizontal. If your loop is too short, the foundation will be tight and you'll find it difficult to insert your hook for the next stitch.

Repeat steps 3 and 4 to complete the stitch: Yarn over, draw through 1 loop on the hook (to form the chain), yarn over, and draw through 2 loops on the hook (to form the single crochet).

You can make other chainless foundations, such as foundation double crochet (fdc) and foundation half double crochet (fhdc), in the same way: Yarn over, draw up a loop in the "chain" at the bottom of the previous stitch, draw through 1 loop to make the next "chain," and complete the stitch as usual.

Linked Stitches

You might have noticed that tall crochet stitches have a vertical gap between each stitch that can make your fabric look gappy. Linked stitches close those gaps and produce a smooth, solid fabric—even with the tallest stitches.

You can link any stitch taller than a single crochet by replacing the initial yarn over(s) at the beginning of the stitch with a loop that links the stitch to the previous stitch. With linked stitches, you don't count the turning chain as a stitch. This example uses linked double crochet (ldc) stitches.

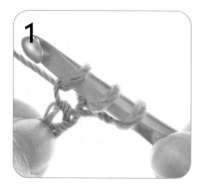

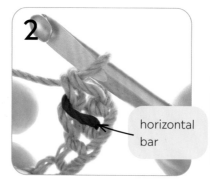

horizontal bar

Make a foundation chain of the required number of stitches plus 2. Insert your hook into the 2nd ch from the hook, yarn over, and draw up a loop. Insert your hook into the next ch, yarn over, and draw up a loop. You now have 3 loops on your hook.

Work the rest of the stitch as a standard dc: (yarn over and draw through 2 loops on the hook) twice to complete the first ldc stitch. The stitch has a horizontal bar halfway up the post. This is the link point for the next stitch.

Insert your hook from top to bottom under the horizontal bar.

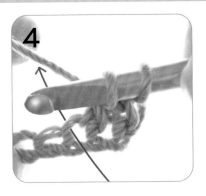

4

Yarn over, draw up a loop (this loop on the hook replaces the yarn over at the start of a dc), and insert your hook into the next chain.

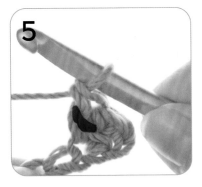

5

Complete the dc: Yarn over and draw up a loop, (yarn over and draw through 2 loops) twice. Repeat steps 3 through 5 for each stitch across the row.

6

To begin a new row, ch 2, and turn your work. Insert your hook into the 2nd ch from the hook, yarn over, and draw up a loop. Insert your hook into the 1st stitch (at the base of the chain), and repeat step 5 to complete the ldc.

7

The bars form a line across the front of each row.

For each additional ldc, draw up a loop in the horizontal bar of the previous ldc, insert your hook into the next st, yarn over, and draw up a loop, (yarn over and draw through 2 loops) twice. Don't crochet into the end turning chain.

You can link any tall stitches in this way—just replace each yarn over at the beginning of the stitch with a linked loop and complete the stitch as usual. For example, to make a linked triple (treble) crochet, draw up a loop in each of the horizontal bars one-third and two-thirds down the previous stitch (or the 2nd and 3rd chs of a ch3 turning chain) to begin the stitch. To eliminate the gap between the turning chain and the next stitch of double and triple crochets, link the next stitch to the turning chain.

Use these horizontal bars to make linked tr stitches.

Practice Project 5:

Pretty
Headband

This lovely headband is good practice for making chainless foundation stitches. It's quick to make and it's a great way to use up leftover yarn.

To make an extra-small or extra-large headband, reduce or increase the number of fsc stitches by a multiple of 3 and follow the remainder of the pattern as written.

Basic Measurements

About 17 inches (43cm) long, excluding ties, and 1½ inches (4cm) wide. One size fits all—the ties make it adjustable.

Yarn

About 25 yards (23m) worsted weight yarn. Shown in Knit Picks Shine Worsted, 60% cotton, 40% plant fiber.

Hook

U.S. I/9 (5.5mm)

Other Supplies

Scissors

Special Stitches

V st: (dc, ch 2, dc) in specified st.

Foundation sc (fsc): *1st fsc st:* ch 2 (doesn't count as st), insert hook into 2nd ch from hook and draw up a loop, YO and draw through 1 loop on hook (to form the ch), YO and draw through both loops on hook (to form the sc). (1 fsc completed)

Subsequent fsc sts: Work each st under the 2 loops that form the ch at the bottom of the previous st. Insert hook under both loops of the ch, draw up a loop, YO and draw through 1 loop on hook (to form the ch), YO and draw through both loops on hook (to form the sc).

New Techniques

Chainless Foundations (page 160)

V Stitch (page 152)

Reading Charted Stitch Diagrams (page 94)

Stitch Diagram

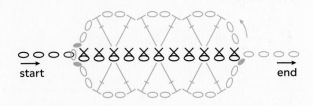

This stitch diagram shows both ends of the headband (with the chain ties shortened) plus one standard repeat.

Ch 27, fsc in 2nd ch from hook, make 56 more fsc sts.

First side: ch 2, turn, sk 1st 2 sts, V st in next st, *sk next 2 sts, V st in next st; rep from * to last 2 sts, ch 2, sk next st, sl st in last st.

Ch 1, rotate piece so you can work into the bottom of the fsc sts, passing the working yarn strand underneath the headband.

Second side: sl st in 1st st, ch 2, sk next st, V st in next st, *sk next 2 sts, V st in next st; rep from * to last 2 sts, ch 2, sk next st, sl st in last st.

Ch 25.

Fasten off and, for extra security, tie an extra knot at each end, over the top of the slipknot and fastening-off knot. Snip the remaining yarn tails to ¼ inch (0.5cm) beyond the knots.

Combination Stitches

Cluster Stitches

Many combination stitches can be called "clusters," but a basic cluster stitch is formed by crocheting several incomplete tall stitches and then joining together all the stitches at the top. This creates a triangular stitch that's wide at the bottom and narrow at the top.

You can use cluster stitches as decreases—or in combination with chains or other stitches so the stitch count isn't reduced—to form stitch patterns. Clusters can be made from any number of stitches. Your pattern gives the details for the specific type of cluster required. Here we learn a basic 4-dc cluster.

Yarn over, insert your hook into the next stitch, and draw up a loop.

Yarn over and draw through 2 loops on the hook. (You now have 2 loops on the hook.)

3

Instead of completing the dc, yarn over, insert your hook into the next stitch, and draw up a loop.

4

Yarn over and draw through 2 loops on the hook. (You now have 3 loops on the hook.)

5

Repeat steps 3 and 4 twice more to make the third and fourth incomplete dc stitches. Each repeat leaves you with 1 more loop remaining on the hook. (You now have 5 loops on the hook.)

6

Yarn over and draw through all 5 loops on the hook to complete the cluster.

Bobble Stitches

You create bobble stitches by crocheting several incomplete tall stitches into a single base stitch and then joining together all the stitches at the top. This creates a single bobble stitch that stands out from the fabric.

Bobbles can be made from any number of double crochet or taller stitches. Your pattern gives the details for the specific type of bobble required in that pattern. Here we learn the basic 4 dc bobble.

Because the bobble naturally pops out to the back of your work as you crochet, bobbles are usually worked on wrong-side rows so they stand out on the front of the finished piece.

Yarn over, insert your hook into the next stitch, and draw up a loop.

Yarn over and draw through 2 loops on the hook. (You now have 2 loops on the hook.)

3

Instead of completing the dc, yarn over, insert your hook into the same stitch, and draw up a loop.

4

Yarn over and draw through 2 loops on the hook. (You now have 3 loops on the hook.)

5

Repeat steps 3 and 4 twice more to make the third and fourth incomplete dc stitches. Each repeat leaves you with 1 more loop remaining on the hook. (You now have 5 loops on the hook.)

6

Yarn over and draw through all 5 loops on the hook to complete the bobble.

Puff Stitches

A puff stitch is formed by crocheting several incomplete half double crochet stitches into a single base stitch and then joining together all the stitches at the top. Each loop is drawn up farther than usual, so the resulting stitch is smooth and puffy.

Puff stitches look very similar from the front and back, and they create a reversible fabric with a soft, cushioned texture. You can make puffs from any number of half double crochet stitches. Your pattern will tell you the specific type of puff required. Here we learn a basic 3-hdc puff.

Work puff stitches *loosely* and draw up your hook to extend the loops. If you don't keep your loops long and loose, you'll find it difficult to draw your hook through all the loops at the end and the resulting puff stitch will be small and not very puffy. But even with long, loose loops, the final step can be tricky. Try gently holding the base of the wraps between your left forefinger and thumb to provide some support as you draw the hook through. With practice, you should be able to pull your hook through all the wraps in one smooth move.

Yarn over, insert your hook into the next stitch, and draw up a loop. (You now have 3 loops on your hook.)

Draw the loop up to the height of your previous stitch so your hook is horizontal.

3

Keep these extra-long loops intact by holding them in place on your hook with your right forefinger as you complete the remaining steps of the stitch.

4

Yarn over, and keeping your tension loose, insert your hook into the same stitch, yarn over, and draw up another loop. (You now have 5 loops on the hook.)

5

Again, draw up the loop to the height of your previous stitch.

6

Repeat steps 4 and 5 to make the third incomplete hdc stitch and draw it up to the height of the previous stitch. (You now have 7 loops on the hook.)

7

Yarn over and draw through all 7 loops on the hook to complete the puff.

Popcorn Stitches

You create a popcorn stitch by crocheting several tall stitches into a single base stitch and then joining together the first and last stitches at the top with a chain. This creates a single stitch that "pops" dramatically from the fabric.

Popcorns can be made from any number of double crochet or taller stitches. Your pattern should give the details for the specific type of popcorn required. Here we learn a basic 4-dc popcorn.

Popcorn stitches pop out to the front of the work as you crochet. Therefore, popcorns are usually worked on right side rows so they stand out on the front of the finished piece.

Work 4 dc stitches into the next stitch.

Draw the working loop on your hook longer and remove your hook from the loop.

3

Insert your hook from front to back under both loops of the first dc stitch you made.

4

Pick up the working loop on your hook and draw it back to the normal size.

5

Draw up the loop through the first stitch to complete the popcorn. The tops of the first and last stitches are now drawn together.

Some patterns specify that the popcorn be closed with a ch 1 as a final step after drawing the working loop through to the front. Check your pattern to see if this chain is included as part of the popcorn stitch.

Puff Stitch
Scarf

Practice making perfect puff stitches with this fun scarf! Worked in a finer yarn, the scarf is warm and squishy without being overly thick. Remember to keep your puff stitches loose.

To ensure you haven't lost or gained a stitch, check the edges of your rows. They should alternate between having a space at each edge of the row (Row 3) and a puff at each edge of the row (Row 4).

To modify the scarf's width, begin with a foundation chain of any multiple of 2 stitches and then follow the rest of the pattern as written.

New Techniques
Puff Stitches (page 172)

Measurements

Approximately 5 inches (13cm) wide by 60 inches (150cm) long. It's easy to add more rows to make the scarf as long as you like.

Yarn

About 300 yards (275m) sport weight yarn. Shown in Knit Picks Andean Treasure, 100% baby alpaca.

Gauge

9½ rows and 8 puffs = 4 inches (10cm). Gauge isn't critical for this project, although a different gauge will affect the final dimensions of the scarf. The row gauge is very dependent on the length of the loops you use to make your puffs.

Hook

U.S. H/8 (5mm)

Other Supplies

Yarn needle, scissors

Notes

You can make this scarf with a larger hook and thicker yarn for a chunkier result that works up more quickly. Or use a 4- or 5-wrap puff stitch to make the puffs extra puffy with very small gaps between them. But be warned: You'll need a lot more yarn with the 4- or 5-wrap version.

Special Stitch

Puff: YO, insert hook into next st and draw up a loop to the height of the previous st, (YO, insert hook into same st and draw up a loop to the same height) twice, YO and draw through all 7 loops on hook.

Stitch Diagram

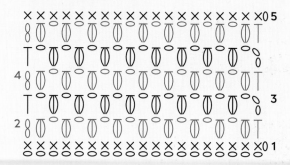

Ch 20 loosely (or use a hook one size larger to make the starting ch).

Row 1: sc in 2nd ch from hook and in each remaining ch. (19 sts)

Row 2: ch 2 (counts as hdc, here and throughout), turn, *puff in next st, ch 1, sk next st; rep from * across to last 2 sts, puff in next st, hdc in last st. (9 puff sts)

Row 3: ch 3 (counts as hdc + ch 1), turn, sk next puff, *puff in next ch1-sp, ch 1, sk next puff; rep from * across to last st, hdc in top of t-ch. (8 puff sts)

Row 4: ch 2, turn, *puff in next ch1-sp, ch 1, sk next puff; rep from * across to t-ch, puff in t-ch space, hdc in 2nd ch of t-ch. (9 puff sts)

Repeat Rows 3 and 4 until the scarf is 60 inches (150cm) long or as many times as desired, ending with a Row 4.

Row 5: ch 1, turn, sc in next st, *sc in next puff, sc in next ch1-sp; rep from * across to last 2 sts, sc in next puff, sc in top of t-ch. (19 sts)

Fasten off and weave in the ends.

Squares and Motifs

All About Motifs

A *motif* is a crocheted shape, such as a square or triangle, that's usually combined into larger pieces to create afghans, shawls, bags, garments, and more.

An individual motif is fast to crochet, portable, and a good way to use up scraps of leftover yarn. Squares are the most common shape of motif because they're easy to combine into different items. You can use one row of joined squares as a scarf or add more rows to create any size and shape of blanket. Just keep adding more squares until you have a rectangle as large as you need.

You can make motifs with any weight of yarn and an appropriately sized hook. Use the hook size recommendation on the yarn's ball band as a starting point and move up to a larger hook if the result is stiffer and denser than you'd like.

Starting a Motif

Motifs are almost always worked in the round, from the center out, without turning your work between rounds. This means that no matter the shape of the finished motif, it usually starts out as a circle.

Each motif is started by working into a starting ring—either a magic ring or a loop of chain stitches. You work all the stitches of Round 1 into this ring and then join the round into a complete circle. As the motif progresses with the subsequent rounds, the square (or triangular, hexagonal, etc.) shape begins to emerge.

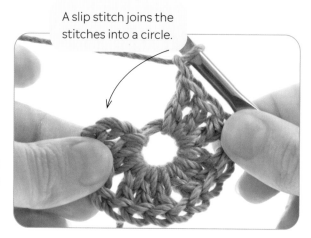

A slip stitch joins the stitches into a circle.

Starting New Rounds

Motifs are often worked with a different color in every round or a pair of colors that alternate with each round. To get the neatest result, rotate your work before you begin each new round so you fasten on with the new yarn on a different side of the shape each time. As your motif grows, the yarn ends and turning chains will be scattered all around the motif instead of being concentrated on one side, where they'd be more noticeable.

To begin each additional round, fasten on by drawing up a loop of the new color of yarn in the specified stitch or space. Crochet over the starting tail with your next stitches to lock the tail in place.

If you want to continue the next round with the same color, don't fasten off. Slip stitch across the top edge until you reach the starting point for the next round and begin the starting chain for that round.

Motif Tips

As you begin each round, crochet over the starting tail from the new round. When you reach the end tail from the previous round, crochet over that too. That way, your yarn tails will be partially woven in before you even pick up your yarn needle!

If you're making motifs in a variety of colors, use the same color to crochet the last round of every motif. Then use this same color when you stitch or crochet the motifs together and the joins will be almost invisible.

You can make larger, even blanket-sized motifs by continuing in the established pattern for as many rounds as you want. With oversized motifs like this, you might notice that the pattern begins to twist as it grows because each crochet stitch sits slightly to the right of the stitch below it. If you notice your motifs start to skew, simply turn your work by flipping it over before you fasten on to begin each new round.

Don't worry if your motifs look rounded at the corners when you finish crocheting them. Joining them into a larger piece coaxes each one into the right shape. For the neatest result in your finished piece, pin each motif into the same size and shape before you join them and then spray or steam block them. This sets the motifs in the correct shape, makes the corners look crisp, and removes any curling.

Granny Squares

The granny square is one of the most recognizable classic crochet motifs. It's an easy pattern to learn and you can change the look by making it in alternating colors or using a different color for each round. (It's a perfect way to use all your yarn scraps!)

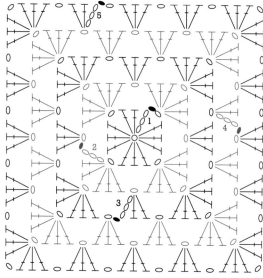

Make a magic ring (or ch 4 and join with sl st into a ring).

Rnd 1: ch 3 (counts as dc, here and throughout); working into the ring: 2 dc, ch 1, (3 dc, ch 1) 3 times. If you're using a magic ring, draw the ring closed. Join with sl st to top of ch 3 and fasten off.

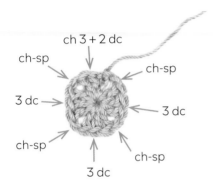

Rnd 2: fasten on with next yarn at any ch-sp. Ch 3, (2 dc, ch 1, 3 dc) in same ch-sp, ch 1, (3 dc, ch 1, 3 dc, ch 1) in next 3 ch-sps. Join with sl st to top of ch 3 and fasten off.

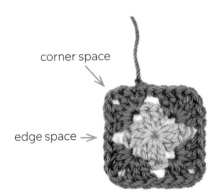

Rnd 3: fasten on with next yarn at any edge ch-sp. Ch 3, 2 dc in same ch-sp, ch 1, *(3 dc, ch 1, 3 dc, ch 1) in next corner ch-sp, 3 dc in next edge ch-sp, ch 1; rep from * twice more, (3 dc, ch 1, 3 dc, ch 1) in last corner ch-sp. Join with sl st to top of ch 3 and fasten off.

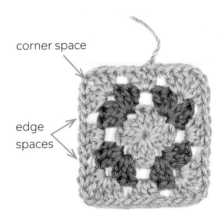

General pattern for all further rounds: fasten on at any edge ch-sp. Ch 3, 2 dc in same ch-sp, ch 1. Make (3 dc, ch 1) in each edge space and rep (3 dc, ch 1) twice in each corner space. Join with sl st to top of ch 3 and fasten off.

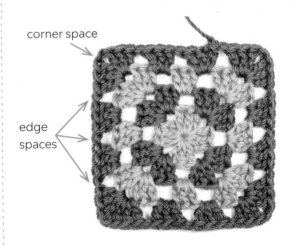

Solid Squares

With this solid variation of a granny square, you work into every stitch instead of splitting into the standard 3 dc clusters. The result is a solid square with a pattern of holes radiating out to each corner.

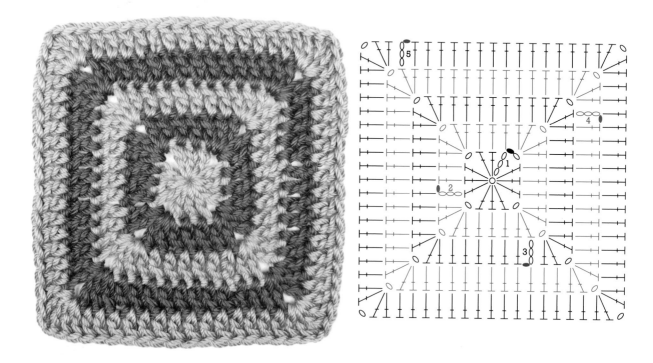

It's easy to accidentally skip the first stitch after each ch-sp. The sideways V at the top of each stitch sits slightly to the *right* of the post of that stitch, so the stitches crammed into the ch-sp might also partially cover the V at the top of the next stitch. If this happens, snug those stitches back to the right to expose the V so you can crochet into it. Check that you haven't lost a stitch by counting the dc stitches along each side of the square. This number increases by 4 with every round, so you should have 7 in Round 2, 11 in Round 3, 15 in Round 4, etc.

Make a magic ring (or ch 4 and join with sl st into a ring).

Rnd 1: ch 3 (counts as dc, here and throughout); working into the ring: 2 dc, ch 1, (3 dc, ch 1) 3 times. If you're using a magic ring, draw the ring closed. Join with sl st to top of ch 3 and fasten off.

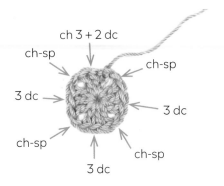

Rnd 2: fasten on with next yarn at any st immediately preceding a ch-sp. Ch 3, (2 dc, ch 1, 2 dc) in next ch-sp, *dc in next 3 sts, (2 dc, ch 1, 2 dc) in next ch-sp; rep from * twice more, dc in next 2 sts. Join with sl st to top of ch 3 and fasten off.

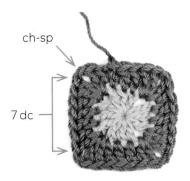

Rnd 3: fasten on with next yarn at any st immediately preceding a ch-sp. Ch 3, (2 dc, ch 1, 2 dc) in next ch-sp, *dc in next 7 sts, (2 dc, ch 1, 2 dc) in next ch-sp; rep from * twice more, dc in next 6 sts. Join with sl st to top of ch 3 and fasten off.

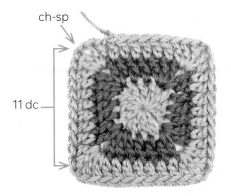

General pattern for all further rounds: fasten on at any st. Ch 3. Dc in each st and make (2 dc, ch 1, 2 dc) in each ch-sp. Join with sl st to top of ch 3 and fasten off.

Circle in a Square

This motif starts out as a circle but transforms into a square—making the finished blocks perfect for stitching together into an afghan! To make the circles pop, crochet Rounds 1 through 3 (the circle) in one color and Rounds 4 and 5 in a different color.

Unlike the other motifs in this chapter, which you can stop at any point, this motif is only complete when it has 5 or more rounds. Rounds 1 through 3 form the center circle and round 4 is a transitional round. From round 5 onward, the motif becomes a standard granny square.

Make a magic ring (or ch 4 and join with sl st into a ring).

Rnd 1: ch 3 (counts as dc, here and throughout), 11 dc into ring. If you're using a magic ring, draw the ring closed. Join with sl st to top of ch 3 and fasten off.

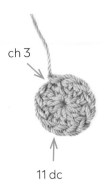

ch 3

11 dc

Rnd 2: fasten on with next yarn at any stitch. Ch 3, dc in same st, ch 1, (2 dc, ch 1) in next 11 sts. Join with sl st to top of ch 3 and fasten off.

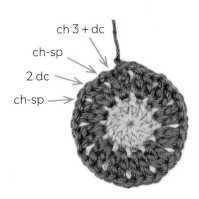

ch 3 + dc

ch-sp

2 dc

ch-sp

Rnd 3: fasten on with next yarn at any ch-sp. Ch 3, 2 dc in same ch-sp, ch 1, (3 dc, ch 1) in next 11 ch-sps. Join with sl st to top of ch 3 and fasten off.

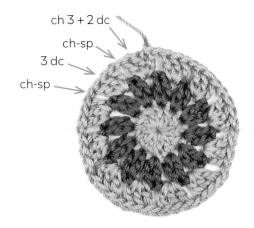

ch 3 + 2 dc

ch-sp

3 dc

ch-sp

Rnd 4: fasten on with next yarn at any ch-sp. Ch 3, 2 dc in same ch-sp, ch 1, 3 dc in next ch-sp, ch 1, *(3 dc, ch 1, 3 dc, ch 1) in next ch-sp, (3 dc, ch 1) in next 2 ch-sps; rep from * twice more, (3 dc, ch 1, 3 dc, ch 1) in next ch-sp. Join with sl st to top of ch 3 and fasten off.

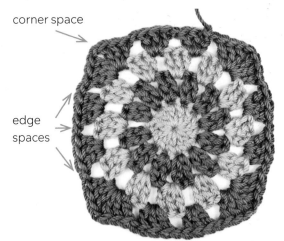

corner space

edge spaces

General pattern for all further rounds: fasten on at any noncorner ch-sp. Ch 3, 2 dc in same ch-sp, ch 1. Make (3 dc, ch 1) in each edge space and rep (3 dc, ch 1) twice in each corner space. Join with sl st to top of ch 3 and fasten off.

Granny Triangles

By removing a corner and adding an extra stitch to each cluster, you can change a granny square into a granny triangle. You can piece these together into an afghan or they're perfect for a colorful bunting!

Make a magic ring (or ch 4 and join with sl st into a ring).

Rnd 1: ch 3 (counts as dc, here and throughout); working into the ring: 3 dc, ch 2, (4 dc, ch 2) twice. If you're using a magic ring, draw the ring closed. Join with sl st to top of ch 3 and fasten off.

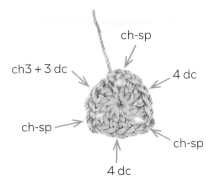

Rnd 2: fasten on with next yarn at any ch-sp. Ch 3, (3 dc, ch 2, 4 dc) in same ch-sp, ch 1, (4 dc, ch 2, 4 dc, ch 1) in next 2 ch-sps. Join with sl st to top of ch 3 and fasten off.

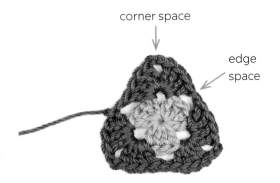

Rnd 3: fasten on with next yarn at any edge ch-sp. Ch 3, 3 dc in same ch-sp, ch 1, *(4 dc, ch 2, 4 dc, ch 1) in next corner ch-sp, 4 dc in next edge ch-sp, ch 1; rep from * once more, (4 dc, ch 2, 4 dc, ch 1) in last corner ch-sp. Join with sl st to top of ch 3 and fasten off.

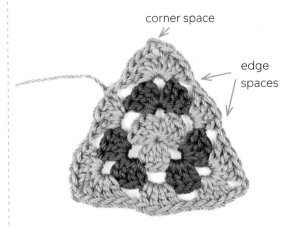

General pattern for all further rounds: fasten on at any edge ch-sp. Ch 3, 3 dc in same ch-sp, ch 1. Make (4 dc, ch 1) in each edge space and (4 dc, ch 2, 4 dc, ch 1) in each corner space. Join with sl st to top of ch 3 and fasten off.

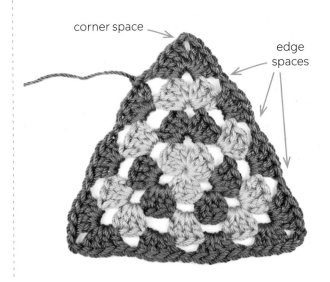

Granny Hexagons

By adding two more corners and removing a stitch from each cluster, you can turn a granny square into a granny-style hexagon. When pieced together, these make a gorgeous afghan.

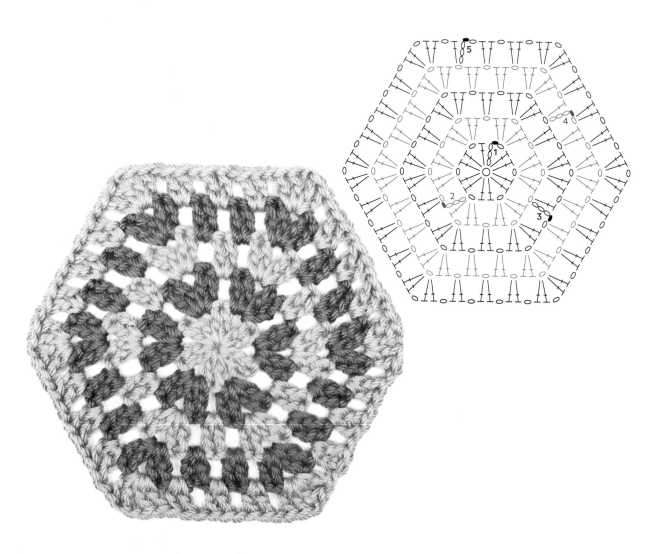

Make a magic ring (or ch 4 and join with sl st into a ring).

Rnd 1: ch 3 (counts as dc, here and throughout); working into the ring: dc, ch 1, (2 dc, ch 1) 5 times. If you're using a magic ring, draw the ring closed. Join with sl st to top of ch 3 and fasten off.

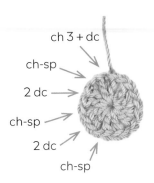

ch 3 + dc

ch-sp

2 dc

ch-sp

2 dc

ch-sp

Rnd 2: fasten on with next yarn at any ch-sp. Ch 3, (dc, ch 1, 2 dc) in same ch-sp, ch 1, (2 dc, ch 1, 2 dc, ch 1) in next 5 ch-sps. Join with sl st to top of ch 3 and fasten off.

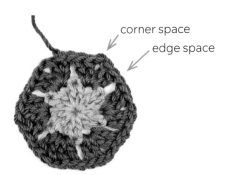

corner space

edge space

Rnd 3: fasten on with next yarn at any edge ch-sp. Ch 3, dc in same ch-sp, ch 1, *(2 dc, ch 1, 2 dc, ch 1) in next corner ch-sp, 2 dc in next edge ch-sp, ch 1; rep from * 4 times more, (2 dc, ch 1, 2 dc, ch 1) in last corner ch-sp. Join with sl st to top of ch 3 and fasten off.

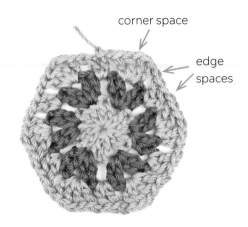

corner space

edge spaces

General pattern for all further rounds: fasten on at any edge ch-sp. Ch 3, dc in same ch-sp, ch 1. Make (2 dc, ch 1) in each edge space and rep (2 dc, ch 1) twice in each corner space. Join with sl st to top of ch 3 and fasten off.

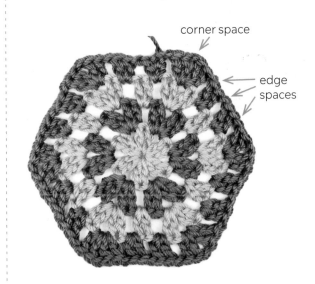

corner space

edge spaces

Edgings and Adornments

Flowers

Pretty crocheted flowers are quick and easy to make, and they're a fun way to add a decorative touch to other projects. You can stitch them directly onto your other crocheted pieces as embellishments or you can sew a pin back onto the wrong side to make a removable flower brooch.

Make these flowers with any size of yarn you like and an appropriate hook for the yarn. I used worsted weight yarn and a U.S. I/9 (5.5mm) hook. The flowers shown measure about 2½ inches (6cm) across.

Simple Flower

Make a magic ring, ch 1.

Rnd 1: (sc in magic ring, ch 2) 6 times. Pull the ring closed and join with sl st to 1st sc.

Rnd 2: (sl st, ch 2, 2 dc, ch 2, sl st) in each ch2-sp. (6 petals made)

Fasten off and weave in the ends or use the ends to stitch the flower to something as an embellishment.

Double Flower

This flower is worked in a continuous spiral. Don't join at the end of the round unless the pattern specifies it.

Make a magic ring, ch 1.

Rnd 1: 6 sc in magic ring. Pull the ring closed. (6 sts)

Rnd 2: (ch 2, dc in front loop of next st, ch 2, sl st in front loop of *same* st) 6 times. (6 petals made)

Fold the petals forward to expose the unworked back loops of the stitches of Round 1.

You'll be working into these back loops in Round 3.

Rnd 3: (ch 1, dc in next st) 6 times, sl st into 1st ch1-sp. (6 dcs made)

Rnd 4: ch 2, 2 dc in same ch1-sp (at base of ch), ch 2, sl st in same ch1-sp, (ch 2, 2 dc in next ch1-sp, ch 2, sl st in same ch1-sp) 5 times. (6 petals made)

Fasten off and weave in the ends or use the ends to stitch the flower to something as an embellishment.

Fringe

Fringe is an easy way to add impact to the ends of a scarf or around the bottom of a shawl.

You can customize fringe in several ways: Use the same color yarn as your project or a contrasting color; add more or fewer strands of yarn in each knot; and vary the space between the knots. You can sometimes also avoid weaving in your yarn ends by incorporating them into the fringe.

For a small project like a scarf, you can calculate how many strands of yarn you'll need to make all the fringe and cut it all at once. For larger projects like a fringed shawl, it's easier to cut a couple dozen strands at a time, tie them on, and cut more strands as you need them.

Wrap your yarn loosely around a piece of cardboard about ½ to 1 inch (1.5 to 2.5cm) longer than the length of the desired fringe. The extra length will form the knot, so you'll need more length if you use thicker yarn or more strands per knot.

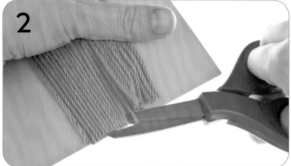

Cut all the strands of yarn across the bottom. Each yarn strand formed will now be the same length.

3

Each length of yarn will form 2 strands in the knot. Decide how many strands to include in each knot (I've used 3 here), hold the strands together, and fold them in half.

4

Insert a crochet hook from back to front through the edge of your project and hook the midpoint of all the folded fringe strands.

5

Draw the yarn loop back through the edge and enlarge it until you can reach through the loop with your thumb and forefinger.

6

Pull the yarn ends through the loop. You can do this with your crochet hook, but especially with thicker fringes, you might find it difficult to catch all the strands with the hook. Pull to tighten the knot.

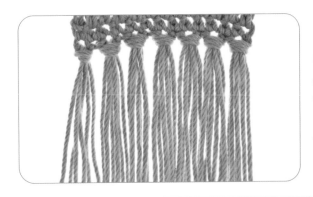

Repeat steps 3 through 6 to make equally spaced fringe knots along the edge of your work. When you're finished, straighten the bottom edge of the fringe by trimming off any extra-long yarn strands.

Reverse Single Crochet

Reverse single crochet (rsc), also known as *crab stitch*, creates a sturdy, nonstretchy, twisted-cord edging.

As the name implies, this stitch is a single crochet stitch worked in the reverse direction. Instead of working from right to left across the row, you work from left to right and begin each new stitch by inserting your hook into the stitch to the *right* of the current stitch. Working this way twists your stitches so the Vs are hidden and the edge is a neatly finished row of tiny bobbles. You can't crochet back into rsc stitches, so reserve this technique for the final row or round of a piece.

Here's how to make a reverse single crochet edging.

Fasten on at any point along the edge and ch 1. To begin each rsc, you work into the *previous* stitch—the stitch to the right of your current stitch.

Insert your hook from front to back into the previous stitch.

Each rsc stitch should look like a small individual knot or bobble, but if you work too quickly, your yarn can snag around the last stitch you made and the two stitches will tangle together. If this happens, unravel the stitch you just made and try again.

3

Keep your hook and working yarn to the right of the previous stitch so the working yarn doesn't get caught up.

Yarn over and draw up a loop, keeping the throat of your hook facing toward the left.

Don't twist your hook like this.

These stitches are wrong.

If you were to twist the hook as you draw up this loop, you'd end up with a mirror-image single crochet stitch instead of a reverse single crochet.

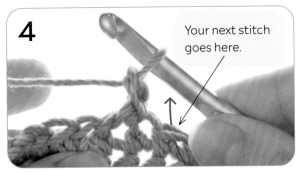

4

Your next stitch goes here.

Complete the rsc in the same way as a standard sc: Yarn over and draw through both loops on the hook.

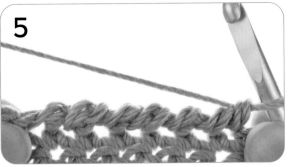

5

Working backward around the edge, rsc in each st around.

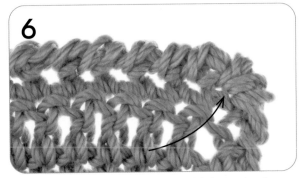

6

At a corner, work as you would for a single crochet edging by making 3 rsc stitches into the corner stitch.

If you're working all the way around an edge, rsc into the stitch where you fastened on and then fasten off.

Picot Edging

A picot edging gives a pretty and delicate finish and is often used to edge lacy pieces and garments for women and children.

A picot is a tiny loop of chain stitches that sits on top of the previous stitch and creates a small round or pointed loop at the edge of a piece or within a lace pattern. Here's how to make a picot edging.

Fasten on in any stitch and ch 1. Sc into the first stitch and then ch 3.

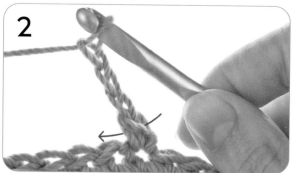

Work into the front loop and the left vertical bar of the stitch at the base of this chain.

Complete the picot with a sl st: Insert your hook through the front loop and left vertical bar of the sc below, draw up a loop, and draw it through the loop on the hook.

Sc in the next 3 stitches and then ch 3 to begin the next picot.

5

Complete the picot with a sl st through the front loop and left vertical bar of the sc at the base of the chain.

6

The completed picot edging follows this pattern: *sc in next st, ch 3, sl st into front loop and left vertical bar of sc at base of ch, sc in next 2 sts; rep from * for as many times as required.

7

3 sc

At a corner, work as you would for a plain sc edging, making 3 sc into the corner stitch. Continue to count your stitches as you go and make another picot after every 3 stitches.

Picots can be formed from various chain lengths or in different ways, and each variation creates a subtly new shape. An *open picot* is a loop of chain stitches; a *closed picot* joins the end of the chain loop to its start with a slip stitch—either into the base stitch (as shown here) or into the first chain stitch. If you're following a pattern, check the description to be sure you're using the intended form of picot.

If you're working all the way around an edge, join with a sl st to the first sc where you fastened on or use an invisible finish for a smoother join.

This picot edging is worked over a multiple of 3 stitches, but to fit into the number of stitches at the edge of your project, you could space your picots closer together or farther apart by reducing or increasing the number of sc stitches between each picot.

Scalloped Edging

Shell stitches create a pretty scalloped edging. You can use any shape and size of shell you want, but the most common scalloped edging uses a 5 dc shell.

To make a 5-dc shell scalloped edging:

Fasten on at the first stitch and ch 1. Sc into the first stitch.

Skip the next 2 stitches and work 5 dc in the next st.

Skip the next 2 stitches and sc in the next st. (1 scallop made)

The completed scalloped edging follows this pattern: * sk next 2 sts, 5 dc in next st, sk next 2 sts, sc in next st; rep from * as many times as required.

When you come to a corner, you can either have the ends of 2 shells meet at the corner or place the center of a shell there.

Ends Meeting at a Corner

Complete the sc at the end of a shell in the corner stitch. Ch 1 to turn the corner and sc into the corner stitch again as the start of the first shell along the new edge.

Centering a Shell at a Corner

Instead of making a 5 dc shell in the corner stitch, work 8 dc in that stitch so the shell travels around the corner. To continue, skip 2 stitches along the next edge and sc in the following stitch.

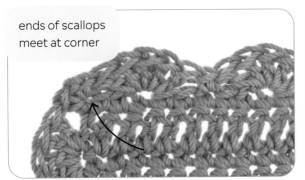

ends of scallops meet at corner

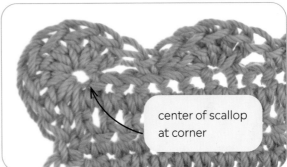

center of scallop at corner

If you're working all the way around an edge, join with a sl st to the first sc where you fastened on or use the invisible finish technique for a smoother join.

A shell is wide and covers several stitches, so your piece should have a multiple of 6 stitches plus 1 along each edge so the stitch pattern works out. If your piece doesn't have the right number of stitches, that's okay. You could crochet a sc edging first and include enough increases in this row, spaced evenly across, to bring each edge up to a multiple of 6 stitches. Or skip only 1 stitch every now and then instead of 2 to increase the stitch count as you complete the shell edging. Provided you spread out these slightly squashed shells across the row, they won't be noticeable in the finished piece.

Intermediate Stitch Gallery

Intermediate Stitch
Patterns

By combining crochet stitches, you can create a huge variety of decorative designs: from lacy, open stitch patterns that make beautiful light shawls and wraps to densely textured patterns perfect for wonderfully warm blankets.

Diamond Fans

Special Stitch

 V st: (dc, ch 1, dc) in specified st.

Ch a multiple of 4 sts plus 2.

Row 1: sc in 2nd ch from hook, *ch 5, sk next 3 chs, sc in next ch; rep from * across to end.

Row 2: ch 3 (counts as dc), turn, dc in same st, ch 1, *sc in next ch5-sp, ch 1, V st in next sc, ch 1; rep from * across to last ch5-sp, sc in last ch5-sp, ch 1, 2 dc in last sc.

Row 3: ch 1, turn, sc in next st, ch 5, *sc in top of V st, ch 5; rep from * across to end, sc in top of t-ch.

Repeat Rows 2 and 3 for the pattern.

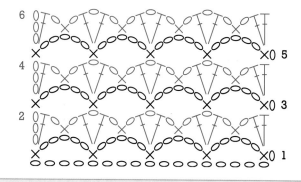

Popcorn Squares

Special Stitch

 Popcorn: Make 4 dc in specified st. Remove hook from working loop, insert hook from front to back in top of 1st dc made, reinsert hook into working loop, and draw through both loops on hook.

Ch a multiple of 4 sts.

Row 1: sc in 2nd ch from hook, *ch 1, sk next ch, sc in next ch; rep from * across to end.

Row 2: ch 3 (counts as dc), turn, dc in next ch1-sp, *ch 1, popcorn in next ch1-sp, ch 1, dc in next ch1-sp; rep from * across to last st, dc in last st.

Row 3: ch 1, turn, sc in next st, ch 1, *sc in next ch1-sp, ch 1; rep from * across to last 2 sts, sk next st, sc in last st.

Repeat Rows 2 and 3 for the pattern.

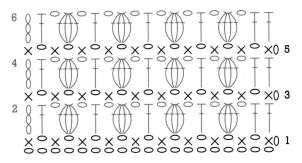

V Bobbles

Special Stitches

 Bobble: (YO, insert hook into st and draw up a loop, YO and draw through 2 loops on hook) twice, YO and draw through all 3 loops on hook.

 V bobble: (bobble, ch 1, bobble) in specified st.

Ch a multiple of 4 sts plus 3.

Row 1: V bobble in 5th ch from hook (unworked chains count as dc), sk next ch, *dc in next ch, sk next ch, V bobble in next ch, sk next ch; rep from * across to last ch, dc in last ch.

Row 2: ch 3 (counts as dc), turn, V bobble in top of next V bobble, *dc in next dc, V bobble in top of next V bobble; rep from * across to last st, dc in top of t-ch.

Repeat Row 2 for the pattern.

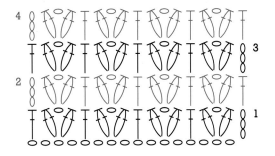

Post Stitch Rib

Ch a multiple of 2 sts.

Row 1: dc in 4th ch from hook (unworked chains count as dc), dc in each remaining ch across.

Row 2: ch 3 (counts as dc), turn, *FPdc in next st, BPdc in next st; rep from * across to last st, dc in top of t-ch.

Repeat Row 2 for the pattern.

Waffle Stitch

Ch a multiple of 3 sts plus 2.

Row 1: dc in 4th ch from hook (unworked chains count as dc), dc in each remaining ch across.

Row 2: ch 3 (counts as dc, here and throughout), turn, *FPdc in next st, dc in next 2 sts; rep from * across to last 2 sts, FPdc in next st, dc in top of t-ch.

Row 3: ch 3, turn, *dc in next st, FPdc in next 2 sts; rep from * across to last 2 sts, dc in next st, dc in top of t-ch.

Repeat Rows 2 and 3 for the pattern.

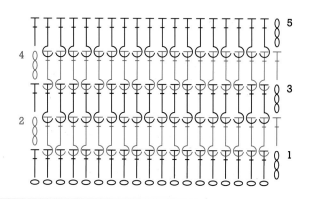

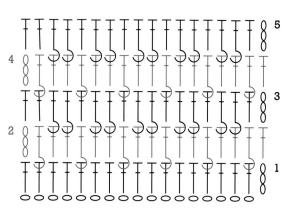

Basket Weave

Ch a multiple of 6 sts plus 4.

Row 1: dc in 4th ch from hook (unworked chains count as dc), dc in each remaining ch across.

Row 2: ch 3 (counts as dc, here and throughout), turn, *FPdc in next 3 sts, BPdc in next 3 sts; rep from * across to last st, dc in top of t-ch.

Row 3: rep Row 2.

Row 4: ch 3, turn, *BPdc in next 3 sts, FPdc in next 3 sts; rep from * across to last st, dc in top of t-ch.

Row 5: rep Row 4.

Repeat Rows 2 through 5 for the pattern.

Diamond Overlay

Ch a multiple of 6 sts plus 3.

Row 1: sc in 2nd ch from hook and in each remaining ch across.

Row 2: ch 3 (counts as dc, here and throughout), turn, *sk next 2 sts, tr in next st, dc in 2 skipped sts (working behind st just made), sk next st, dc in next 2 sts, tr in skipped st (working in front of sts just made); rep from * across to last st, dc in last st.

Row 3: ch 1, turn, sc in each st across.

Row 4: ch 3, turn, *sk next st, dc in next 2 sts, tr in skipped st (working in front of sts just made), sk next 2 sts, tr in next st, dc in 2 skipped sts (working behind st just made); rep from * across to last st, dc in last st.

Row 5: rep Row 3.

Repeat Rows 2 through 5 for the pattern.

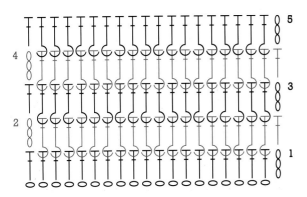

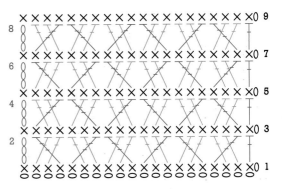

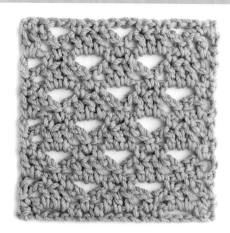

Triangle Spaces

Ch a multiple of 6 sts plus 2.

Row 1: sc in 2nd ch from hook, sc in next ch, ch 3, sk next 3 chs, sc in next ch, *ch 1, sk next ch, sc in next ch, ch 3, sk next 3 chs, sc in next ch; rep from * across to last ch, sc in last ch.

Row 2: ch 1, turn, sc in next st, ch 2, 3 dc in next ch3-sp, *ch 2, sc in next ch1-sp, ch 2, 3 dc in next ch3-sp; rep from * across to last 2 sts, ch 2, sk next st, sc in last st.

Row 3: ch 4 (counts as dc + ch 1), turn, sc in next dc, ch 1, sk next dc, sc in next dc, *ch 3, sc in next dc, ch 1, sk next dc, sc in next dc; rep from * across to end, ch 1, dc in last sc.

Row 4: ch 3 (counts as dc), turn, dc in next ch1-sp, ch 2, sc in next ch1-sp, *ch 2, 3 dc in next ch3-sp, ch 2, sc in next ch1-sp; rep from * across to last space, ch 2, 2 dc in t-ch space.

Row 5: ch 1, turn, sc in next 2 dcs, ch 3, *sc in next dc, ch 1, sk next dc, sc in next dc, ch 3; rep from * across to last 2 sts, sc in next dc, sc in top of t-ch.

Repeat Rows 2 through 5 for the pattern.

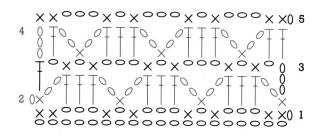

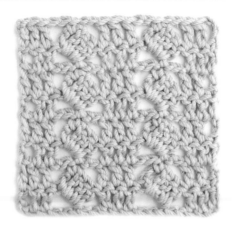

Tumbling Blocks

Special Stitch

To work a stitch around the post of a previous stitch, insert the hook under the stitch (instead of into it) and crochet around it.

Ch a multiple of 8 sts plus 5.

Row 1: dc in 4th ch from hook (unworked chs count as dc), *dc in next ch, sk next 2 chs, dc in next ch, ch 3, 3 dc around post of dc just worked, sk next 2 chs, dc in next 2 chs; rep from * across to last ch, dc in last ch.

Row 2: ch 3 (counts as dc, here and throughout), turn, *dc in next 2 dcs, ch 2, sc in ch3-sp, ch 2, sk next dc, dc in next dc; rep from * across to last 2 sts, dc in next dc, dc in top of t-ch.

Row 3: ch 3, turn, *dc in next 2 dcs, dc in next sc, ch 3, 3 dc around post of dc just worked, dc in next dc; rep from * across to last 2 sts, dc in next dc, dc in top of t-ch.

Repeat Rows 2 and 3 for the pattern.

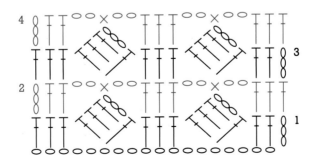

Mini Picot Mesh

Special Stitch

 Picot: ch 3, sl st into front loop and left vertical bar of sc at base of ch.

Ch a multiple of 3 sts plus 2.

Row 1: sc in 2nd ch from hook, *ch 3, sk next 2 chs, sc in next ch, picot; rep from * across to last 3 chs, ch 3, sk next 2 chs, sc in last ch.

Row 2: ch 4 (counts as dc + ch 1), turn, *sc in next ch3-sp, picot, ch 3; rep from * across to last ch3-sp, sc in last ch3-sp, picot, ch 1, dc in last st.

Row 3: ch 1, turn, sc in next st, ch 3, *sc in next ch3-sp, picot, ch 3; rep from * across to end, sc in 3rd ch of t-ch.

Repeat Rows 2 and 3 for the pattern.

You can omit the picots from the final row to give a straighter top edge. And with lacy patterns like this, blocking is essential to open the mesh and really show off the stitch pattern.

Offset Arches

Special Stitches

 Shell: (4 dc, ch 1, 4 dc) in specified st.

 **V st:** (dc, ch 1, dc) in specified st.

Ch a multiple of 8 sts plus 2.

Row 1: sc in 2nd ch from hook, *sk next 3 chs, shell in next ch, sk next 3 chs, sc in next ch; rep from * across to end.

Row 2: ch 3 (counts as dc, here and throughout), turn, dc in same st, ch 2, *sc in top of next shell, ch 2, V st in next sc, ch 2; rep from * across to last shell, sc in top of last shell, ch 2, 2 dc in last sc.

Row 3: ch 3, turn, 4 dc in same st, *sc in next sc, shell in top of next V st; rep from * across to last sc, sc in next sc, 5 dc in top of t-ch.

Row 4: ch 1, turn, sc in next st, ch 2, *V st in next sc, ch 2, sc in top of next shell, ch 2; rep from * across to last sc, V st in last sc, ch 2, sc in top of t-ch.

Row 5: ch 1, turn, sc in next st, *shell in top of next V st, sc in next sc; rep from * across to end.

Repeat Rows 2 through 5 for the pattern, ending on an even-numbered row.

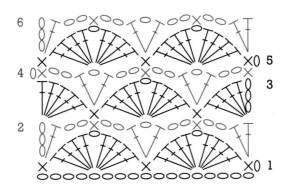

PART 4

A Gallery of Patterns

Flecked
Scarf

Despite its multicolored
appearance, each row of this
scarf is worked in only one
color. It's worked lengthwise,
which means you don't have
any ends to weave. You can
combine them in the fringe!

Measurements

About 4½ inches (11cm) wide and 60 inches (150cm) long, excluding fringe.

Yarn

255 yards (235m) DK (light) weight yarn: 175 yards (160m) main color (MC) and 80 yards (75m) contrast color (CC). Shown in Knit Picks Gloss DK, 70% merino wool, 30% silk.

Gauge

14 rows and 12 sts = 4 inches (10cm) in stitch pattern. Gauge isn't critical for this project, although a different gauge will affect the final dimensions of the scarf. Choose a hook size large enough that your fabric drapes nicely and isn't too stiff.

Hook

U.S. J/10 (6mm)

Other Supplies

Scissors, cardboard template for fringe (optional)

Notes

This pattern also looks great as a narrower scarf. If you make a scarf with 5 rows of CC flecks instead of 7, you might only need a single ball of the main color yarn.

Leave a 6-inch (15cm) tail at the start and end of each row. (You'll work these into the fringe after the scarf is complete.)

Special Stitches

Foundation half double crochet (fhdc):

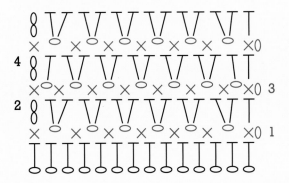

1st fhdc: ch 2 (doesn't count as st), YO, insert hook into 2nd ch from hook and draw up a loop,

YO and draw through 1 loop on hook (to form the ch), YO and draw through all 3 loops on hook (to form the hdc). (1 fhdc completed)

Subsequent fhdcs: Work each st under the 2 loops that form the ch at the bottom of the previous st. YO, insert hook under both loops of the ch, draw up a loop, YO and draw through 1 loop on hook (to form the ch), YO and draw through all 3 loops on hook (to form the hdc).

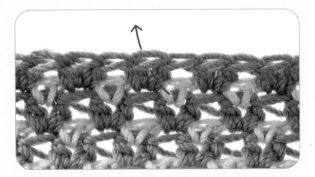

Working between stitches: The CC sts are worked *between* each pair of MC sts in the row below. Insert hook between the posts of the 2 sts, draw up a loop, and complete the st as usual.

Stitch Diagram

A reduced sample of the scarf's stitch pattern.

Flecked Scarf

With **MC**, fhdc 180. (180 sts)

Chainless foundation stitches make a stretchy edge, so your scarf will be perfectly symmetrical. If you don't want to use them, you can work this alternative foundation instead. (You might need to use a hook one size larger for the starting chain to keep it loose.): with **MC**, ch 181, hdc in 3rd ch from hook (unworked chs count as hdc) and in each remaining ch. (180 sts).

Row 1: with **CC**, ch 1, turn, sc in 1st st, ch 1, sk next 2 sts, sc in next sp between sts, *ch 1, sk next sp, sc in next sp; rep from * across to last 3 sts, ch 1, sk next 2 sts, sc in last st.

Row 2: with **MC**, ch 2 (counts as hdc, here and throughout), turn, 2 hdc in each ch1-sp across, hdc in last st.

Row 3: with **CC**, ch 1, turn, sc in 1st st, ch 1, sk next st, sc in next sp between sts, *ch 1, sk next sp, sc in next sp; rep from * across to last 2 sts, ch 1, sk next st, sc in top of t-ch.

Row 4: with **MC**, ch 2, turn, hdc in 1st ch1-sp, 2 hdc in each ch1-sp across to last ch1-sp, hdc in last ch1-sp, hdc in last st.

Repeat Rows 1 through 4 twice more and then repeat Rows 1 and 2 once more.

Fringe (optional):

Measure and cut 8-inch-long (20cm-long) strands of yarn (32 strands of MC and 16 strands of CC)—either with a ruler or by wrapping the yarn loosely around a piece of 4-inch-tall (10cm-tall) cardboard and then cutting all the strands of yarn across the bottom of the cardboard. For a step-by-step tutorial, see Fringe (page 196).

Hold 2 strands of MC and 1 strand of CC together, fold them in half, and knot them through the first stitch at one end of the scarf.

To save weaving in the yarn ends from the scarf, pull each end through the nearest fringe knot as you form it. Trim the ends to match the length of the fringe strands. If you prefer to omit the fringe, use a yarn needle to weave all the ends into the stitches of the same color.

Repeat in each MC row across each short end of the scarf. You should have 8 fringe knots along each end.

Resizing the Pattern

To modify the length of the scarf, fhdc any multiple of 2 stitches (or ch any odd number of stitches) until you reach the desired length. To modify the width, repeat Rows 1 through 4 as many times as desired and then repeat Rows 1 and 2 once more. This will leave you with an odd number of rows of CC flecks, so the overall pattern will be symmetrical.

Cozy
Cowl

With its textured stitch pattern, this cowl will keep you warm and in style without adding too much bulk and thickness. It's also completely reversible.

Measurements

About 21 inches (53cm) around and 9 inches (23cm) tall.

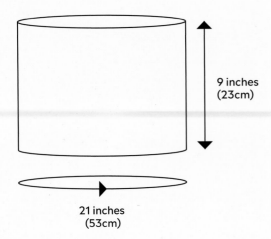

9 inches (23cm)

21 inches (53cm)

Yarn

About 190 yards (175m) DK (light) weight yarn. Shown in Knit Picks Capra Cashmere, 85% merino wool, 15% cashmere.

Gauge

9 rows and 4 (sc, V st) repeats = 4 inches (10cm). Gauge isn't critical for this project, although a different gauge will affect the final dimensions of the cowl.

Hook

U.S. K/10.5 (6.5mm)

Other Supplies

Yarn needle, scissors

Special Stitches

V st: (dc, ch 1, dc) in specified st.

Resizing the Pattern

You can make this cowl as long or short as you like—from a close-fitting pull-on neck warmer to an extra-long cowl you can loop two or three times around your neck. Just repeat Row 2 until you reach the desired length and seam the ends together. To modify the height of the cowl, begin with a foundation chain of any multiple of 4 stitches plus 3. The starting chain is longer than the height of the finished cowl, so to figure out how tall to make the cowl with your yarn and gauge, start by making a swatch of a few rows of the cowl with the standard height. Then decide how many repeats to add to or subtract from your foundation chain to reach the desired height.

Stitch Diagram

A reduced sample of the stitch pattern for the cowl.

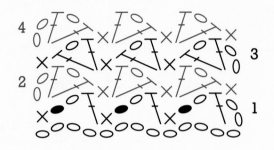

Cozy Cowl

Leaving a 6-inch (15cm) starting tail, ch 39.

Row 1: dc in 3rd ch from hook, ch 1, sk next 2 chs, sl st in next ch, *(sc, dc) in next ch, ch 1, sk next 2 chs, sl st in next ch; rep from * across to last ch, sc in last ch.

Row 2: ch 2, turn, V st in 1st st, *(sc, V st) in next sc; rep from * across to end, sc in t-ch sp.

Repeat Row 2 46 more times or until you reach the desired length. If you modify the length, finish on an even-numbered row so the starting and ending yarn tails are on opposite sides of the cowl.

Fasten off, leaving a 3-foot (1m) yarn tail. Thread the tail through a yarn needle and whip stitch each ch of the starting chain to the corresponding st along the top of the final row, being sure the cowl isn't twisted before you begin joining the ends. For a step-by-step tutorial, see Whip Stitch (page 135). The wavy top and bottom edges align together, making the seam almost invisible.

Block if desired and weave in the ends.

Phone or Tablet
Slipcover

Protect your electronic devices with this stylish, custom-fitted cushioned sleeve. You can easily modify the cover to fit any size and shape of cell phone, tablet, e-reader, MP3 player, or any other flat rectangular device.

The slipcover slides over your device with a smooth, tight fit that stays in place without adding much bulk. The dense fabric protects your screen from scratches and you can answer your phone quickly because the sleeve slides off easily.

Measurements

Custom fit to the size of your device. Samples show a cell phone (5-inch; 12cm screen) and a small tablet (7-inch; 18cm screen).

Yarn

Worsted weight yarn. The quantity required varies depending on the size of your device; you'll need about 40 yards (37m) for a phone cover, 90 yards (82m) for a small tablet cover, and 190 yards (175m) for a large tablet cover. Shown in Knit Picks Shine Worsted, 60% cotton, 40% plant fiber.

Gauge

17 rows and 17 sts = 4 inches (10cm). Gauge isn't critical for this project, as you can fit it to the size of your device.

Hook

U.S. G/7 (4.5mm)

Other Supplies

2 stitch markers, yarn needle, scissors

Notes

This sleeve is worked in a continuous seamless spiral, from the bottom up.

Phone or Tablet Slipcover

Ch 11 (18, 30) or any number so the taut (but not stretched) chain is as long as the width of your device.

If you match the stated gauge, you can calculate the correct starting chain length. For inches, multiply the width by 4. For example, a 5.5-inch-wide device needs a starting chain of $5.5 \times 4 = 22$ chains. For centimeters, multiply the width by 1.6. For example, a 14-centimeter-wide device needs a starting chain of $14 \times 1.6 = 22.4$ (rounded to 22) chains.

Rnd 1: sc in 2nd ch from hook and in each remaining ch to the end, 3 sc in the last ch. Place a stitch marker in the last st worked. Rotate your piece so you can work into the unworked loops at the bottom of the foundation chain: sc in each st to the end, 3 sc in the last st. Place a stitch marker in the last st worked. (24 [38, 62] sts)

Rnd 2: sc in each st until the 1st marked st, 2 sc in marked st, sc in each st until the 2nd marked st, 2 sc in marked st. (26 [40, 64] sts)

From Round 3, you'll work in a continuous spiral without keeping track of how many rounds you make or where the start of the round is. Just keep spiraling around until it's long enough.

To make the beautiful staggered stitch pattern, it's important you crochet into the first of each pair of stitches from the round below and skip the second. If you don't see the diagonal lines forming from round to round, check to be sure you haven't lost or gained a stitch somewhere.

Rnd 3: 2 sc in next st, *sk next st, 2 sc in next st; rep from * until you reach the desired length.

As you start to spiral around, the piece will start to form a cup shape. After about 3 rounds, flip the cup inside out so the right side of your stitches is on the outside. Then check for size to be sure it's a fairly snug fit but not too tight to insert your device.

Depending on how much the sleeve is stretched widthwise to fit your device, it might lose length, so check for length before you fasten off by inserting your phone into the sleeve. To protect the entire phone, the cover might need to be a round longer than you'd expect.

Finishing: When you've reached the right length, flatten the cover so the starting chain lies flat along the bottom edge. Continue in the (skip next st, 2 sc in next st) stitch pattern until you reach one of the side edges of the cover and then skip next st, sl st in next st.

Fasten off (if desired, use an invisible finish in the next stitch to create a smoother join) and weave in the yarn ends.

Handy
Baskets

These nesting baskets are so handy! Keep one by the front door for your keys and pocket change, a couple in the bathroom for soaps and cotton balls, and some on your desk for stationery and crochet notions. Where else can you think of to use them?

Although single crochet stitches are short, there's still space to insert your hook at either side of the post of each stitch so you can work post stitches around them just as you would with any taller stitch. The post stitches give a neat and defined corner at the edge of the basket base.

Measurements

About 4 (5, 6) inches (10 [12.5, 15]cm) across and 2 (2.25, 2.5) inches (5 [5.5, 6]cm) tall.

Yarn

About 70 (105, 150) yards (65 [100, 140]m) worsted weight cotton or cotton blend yarn: 60 (95, 140) yards (55 [90, 130]m) main color (MC) and less than 10 yards (10m) contrast color (CC). Shown in Knit Picks Dishie, 100% cotton.

Gauge

12 rows and 12 sts = 4 inches (10cm), with yarn held doubled. Gauge isn't critical for this project, although a different gauge will affect the final dimensions of the baskets.

Hook

U.S. K/10.5 (6.5mm)

Other Supplies

Stitch marker, yarn needle, scissors

Notes

You work in a continuous spiral, so place a stitch marker in the first stitch of each round and move it up as you begin each new round to be sure you don't lose your place in the pattern.

The side that faces you while you crochet will become the outside of the basket.

You hold the yarn double when crocheting these baskets. Not only does this help make the basket stiff and rigid, but it also means you can use a large hook and stitch these baskets very quickly!

To work with 2 strands of yarn held together, find the yarn end from the center of your ball and hold it together with the yarn end from the outside of the ball so you have 2 strands to work with. For every stitch you crochet, grab both strands of yarn with your hook.

Options: Instead of using 2 strands of the same color yarn, crochet with 2 different colors held together to make a variegated basket. Or for a taller basket, add one or more additional rounds of single crochet before you fasten off to add the contrasting trim. For smaller baskets, crochet these patterns with 1 strand of yarn and a size U.S. H/8 (5mm) hook.

Special Stitch

Back post single crochet (BPsc): insert hook from back to front to back around post of next st, YO and draw up a loop, YO and draw through both loops on hook.

Handy Baskets

With 2 strands of **MC** held together, make a magic ring, ch 1.

Rnd 1: 6 sc in magic ring. Pull the ring closed. (6 sts)

Rnd 2: 2 sc in each st around. (12 sts)

Rnd 3: (2 sc in next st, sc in next st) 6 times. (18 sts)

Rnd 4: (sc in next st, 2 sc in next st, sc in next st) 6 times. (24 sts)

Rnd 5: (2 sc in next st, sc in next 3 sts) 6 times. (30 sts)

Rnd 6: (sc in next 2 sts, 2 sc in next st, sc in next 2 sts) 6 times. (36 sts)

Medium and large baskets only:

Rnd 7: (2 sc in next st, sc in next 5 sts) 6 times. (42 sts)

Rnd 8: (sc in next 3 sts, 2 sc in next st, sc in next 3 sts) 6 times. (48 sts)

Large basket only:

Rnd 9: (2 sc in next st, sc in next 7 sts) 6 times. (54 sts)

Rnd 10: (sc in next 4 sts, 2 sc in next st, sc in next 4 sts) 6 times. (60 sts)

All baskets:

Rnd 11: BPsc in each st around. (36 [48, 60] sts)

Rnd 12: sc in each st around. (36 [48, 60] sts)

Repeat Round 12 an additional 3 [4, 5] times. (36 [48, 60] sts)

Sl st in next st. Join with an invisible finish to disguise the join.

Trim:

Fasten on in the 1st st with 2 strands of **CC** held together, ch 1 (counts as sc), sc in each remaining st around. (36 [48, 60] sts)

Join with an invisible finish, which makes the starting ch 1 appear to be a complete sc stitch.

Repeat the trim for a 2nd round, with 2 strands of **MC** held together.

Finishing:

Weave in the ends. To reduce bulk, where possible, weave in each strand individually through different stitches.

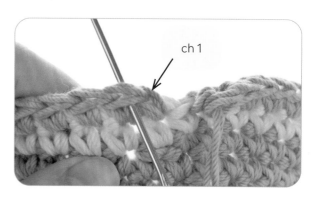

ch 1

To make the join completely invisible, pass the ends from front to back under both loops of the first sc of the round.

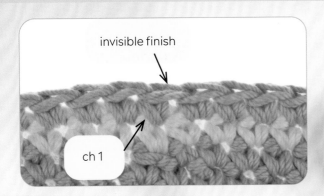

invisible finish

ch 1

Insert the needle under the back loop and back horizontal bar of the final sc of the round and pull tight.

Placemat
and
Coaster Set

The solid, textured design of these placemats and matching coasters will add a little crocheted style to your dining table. Choose a color to complement your décor.

Measurements

Placemat: about 15 inches (38cm) wide and 10 inches (26cm) tall.

Coaster: about 3½ inches (9cm) square.

Yarn

DK (light) cotton or cotton blend yarn, about 210 yards (190m) per placemat and 20 yards (18m) per coaster. Shown in Knit Picks CotLin DK, 70% cotton, 30% linen.

Gauge

14 rows and 15 sts = 4 inches (10cm) in DK yarn. Gauge isn't critical for this project, although a different gauge will affect the final dimensions.

Hook

U.S. G/7 (4.5mm)

Other Supplies

Yarn needle, scissors

Notes

For a slightly larger set, use a worsted weight yarn with a size U.S. H/8 (5mm) or U.S. I/9 (5.5mm) hook.

Special Stitches

Reverse single crochet (rsc): insert hook into previous st, YO and draw up a loop, YO and draw through both loops on hook. (1 rsc completed)

The main pattern is worked over a pair of stitches, with a sc decrease over both stitches and then a dc worked into the same stitch (the 2nd stitch of the pair).

Stitch Diagram

A reduced sample of the stitch pattern for both the placemat and coaster.

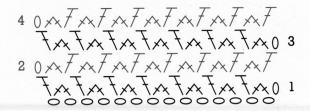

Placemat

Ch 55.

Row 1: sc2tog in 2nd and 3rd chs from hook, dc in same ch, *sc2tog, dc in same ch; rep from * across to end of row. (54 sts)

Row 2: ch 1, turn, *sc2tog, dc in same st; rep from * across to end of row. (54 sts)

Rows 3 through 36: rep Row 2 34 more times or as many times as desired.

Border: don't turn; rsc in each st across the top of each st, 3 rsc in the corner, rsc in the edge of each row. Continue to work around the placemat in this way, making 1 rsc into each st or row edge and 3 rsc in each corner.

Fasten off and weave in the ends.

To modify the size, begin with a foundation chain of an odd number of stitches for the width of the placemat and follow the rest of the pattern for as many rows as you like for the height of the mat.

Coaster

Ch 15.

Row 1: sc2tog in 2nd and 3rd chs from hook, dc in same ch, *sc2tog, dc in same ch; rep from * across to end of row. (14 sts)

Row 2: ch 1, turn, *sc2tog, dc in same st; rep from * across to end of row. (14 sts)

Rows 3 through 10: rep Row 2 8 more times or as many times as needed to make the coaster square.

Border: don't turn; rsc in each st across the top of each st, 3 rsc in the corner, rsc in the edge of each row. Continue to work around the coaster in this way, making 1 rsc into each st or row edge and 3 rsc in each corner.

Fasten off and weave in the ends.

To modify the size, begin with a foundation ch of an odd number of stitches and follow the rest of the pattern for as many rows as needed for the coaster to be square.

For the border on the placemat and coaster, make 1 rsc stitch into the side of each row, making each stitch around each stitch (not into the stitch itself) along the edge. The rsc stitches will be more widely spaced down the sides than along the top and bottom edges, which prevents the placemat/coaster from stretching vertically and keeps it flat.

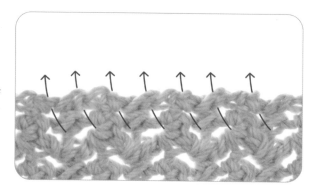

Rolling Waves
Blanket

Crocheting an afghan is the perfect way to spend a cozy winter's evening—the blanket keeps you warm even as you crochet it! This design is gender-neutral and quick to crochet in any three colors of your choice. It would make a perfect gift—if you can bring yourself to part with it.

Measurements

About 48 inches (120cm) wide and 36 inches (90cm) tall.

Yarn

Worsted weight yarn in 3 colors: about 765 yards (700m) of main color (MC) and 330 yards (300m) each of colors A and B. Shown in Knit Picks Brava Worsted, 100% acrylic.

Gauge

8 rows and 12½ sts = 4 inches (10cm). Gauge isn't critical for this project, although a different gauge will affect the final dimensions of the blanket.

Hooks

U.S. I/9 (5.5mm), U.S. J/10 (6mm)

Other Supplies

Yarn needle, scissors

Notes

This pattern also looks lovely with only 2 colors. To do this, simply work all rows of A and B with the same contrast color.

Rows 2 and 3 start with a ch 3 turning chain to prevent a gappy edge. If you chain tightly and your ch 3 edge pulls in, try a ch 4 instead.

Because you cut the yarn after every color stripe, you'll have lots of ends to take care of. You have a few options for dealing with these. For the neatest result, weave the ends of each color into the stitches of the same color. You can speed up your finishing time by working over your ends every time you change color.

Or to avoid generating yarn ends, loosely carry the unworked yarns up the side of the piece until you need them. As you crochet the edging, hide all the carried strands by crocheting over them.

Stitch Diagram

A reduced sample of the blanket's stitch pattern.

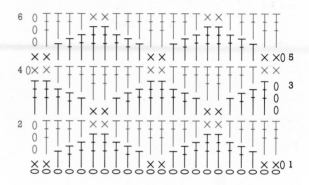

Rolling Waves Blanket

With larger hook and **MC**, ch 143. Change to smaller hook.

Row 1: sc in 2nd ch from hook, *sc in next ch, hdc in next ch, dc in next 2 chs, tr in next 2 chs, dc in next 2 chs, hdc in next ch, sc in next ch; rep from * across to last ch, sc in last ch.

Change to **A**.

Row 2: ch 3 (counts as tr), turn, *tr in next st, dc in next 2 sts, hdc in next st, sc in next 2 sts, hdc in next st, dc in next 2 sts, tr in next st; rep from * across to last st, tr in last st.

Row 3: ch 3 (counts as tr), turn, *tr in next st, dc in next 2 sts, hdc in next st, sc in next 2 sts, hdc in next st, dc in next 2 sts, tr in next st; rep from * across to last st, tr in top of t-ch.

Change to **MC**.

Row 4: ch 1, turn, sc in 1st st, *sc in next st, hdc in next st, dc in next 2 sts, tr in next 2 sts, dc in next 2 sts, hdc in next st, sc in next st; rep from * across to last st, sc in top of t-ch.

Row 5: ch 1, turn, sc in 1st st, *sc in next st, hdc in next st, dc in next 2 sts, tr in next 2 sts, dc in next 2 sts, hdc in next st, sc in next st; rep from * across to last st, sc in last st.

Rows 6 and 7: with **B**, rep Rows 2 and 3.

Rows 8 and 9: with **MC**, rep Rows 4 and 5.

Repeat Rows 2 through 9 an additional 7 times for a total of 8 repeats. Repeat Rows 2 through 8 so you finish with a straight edge worked in MC. Don't fasten off.

Edging: don't turn; ch 2 (counts as dc), work 4 dc in the corner st, and dc evenly down the side edge by working 2 dc in every stripe of MC and approximately 5 dc in every stripe of A or B (or as many as needed for the edge to lie flat).

Work 5 dc in the corner st and dc across the unworked loop(s) of the foundation chain. Work 5 dc in the corner st and dc evenly up the other side as before. Work 5 dc in the final corner and dc across the top of the blanket. Join with sl st to top of ch 2 (or use an invisible finish for a smoother join).

Fasten off and weave in the ends.

Resizing the Pattern

This pattern as written makes a throw or lap afghan, but you can easily adapt the pattern to make any size of blanket. Chain a multiple of 10 + 3 sts to make the width of your blanket and follow the pattern as written. Repeat Rows 2 through 9 as many times as desired and repeat Rows 2 through 8 once more so you finish with a straight edge worked in MC. Work the edging as written.

Solid Stripes
Bag

You create the textured stripes for this bag by using linked stitches that let you complete the tall rows quickly without leaving any gaps or holes that smaller items (like crochet hooks!) could fall through.

Aside from a few stitches to join the short ends of the strap together, this is a no-sew pattern. All the assembly is done by crocheting.

Measurements

Bag: about 8½ inches (22cm) wide and 10½ inches (27cm) tall.

Strap: about 11½ inches (29cm) from the top of the bag to the halfway point.

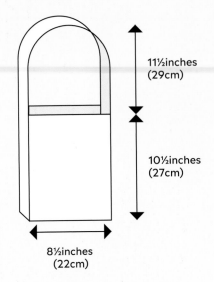

Yarn

320 yards (290m) DK (light) cotton or cotton blend yarn. Shown in Knit Picks CotLin DK, 70% cotton, 30% linen.

Gauge

8 rows = 5 inches (12.5cm) and 19 sts = 4 inches (10cm). Gauge isn't critical for this project, although a different gauge will affect the final dimensions of the bag.

Hook

U.S. H/8 (5mm)

Other Supplies

Yarn needle, scissors, stitch markers

Notes

With linked stitches, the turning chain does **not** count as a stitch.

For this pattern, crochet into the back bumps of the foundation chain. This leaves you with a clear V to work back into when you crochet into the bottom of the chain, which makes assembly easier.

Special Stitch

Linked triple (treble) crochet (ltr): *1st ltr:* insert hook in 2nd ch from hook and draw up a loop, insert hook in 3rd ch from hook and draw up a loop, insert hook in next st and draw up a loop. (YO and draw through 2 loops on hook) 3 times (1st ltr made).

Subsequent ltrs: insert hook down through upper horizontal bar of previous st and draw up a loop, insert hook down through lower horizontal bar of same st and draw up a loop, insert hook in next st and draw up a loop. (YO and draw through 2 loops on hook) 3 times (ltr made).

For a step-by-step tutorial, see Linked Stitches (page 162).

Solid Stripes Bag

Bag front/back (make 2):

Ch 43.

Row 1: Complete 1st ltr in back bump of 2nd, 3rd, and 4th chs from hook, ltr in back bump of each remaining ch. (40 sts)

Row 2: ch 3, turn, complete 1st ltr in 2nd ch, 3rd ch, and 1st st, ltr in each st across. (40 sts)

Rows 3 through 17: rep Row 2.

Fasten off and weave in the ends.

Strap and gusset strip:

Ch 230.

Complete 1st ltr in back bump of 2nd, 3rd, and 4th chs from hook, ltr in back bump of each remaining chain. (227 sts)

Sl st in upper horizontal bar of previous st, sl st in lower horizontal bar of same st, sl st in last ch worked.

Rotate the strip so you can work into the unworked loops at the bottom of the foundation chain: ch 3, complete 1st ltr in 2nd and 3rd ch from hook and in 1st st, ltr in each remaining st. (227 sts)

As you did at the other end, make 3 sl st down the side of the last st worked.

Fasten off and weave in the ends.

Assembly:

Block each piece if desired. I recommend a simple spray blocking to square up the edges and smooth out the stitches. This makes the assembly process easier and gives the bag a more polished appearance. The exact dimensions for the bag aren't critical, but check as you pin to be sure the front and back pieces are the same size as each other.

Join the strip: Ensuring the strip isn't twisted, match the two short ends of the strip, with the right side (the side with the horizontal lines visible from the linked stitches) facing up. Mattress stitch the two short ends of the strip together to form a continuous loop.

Join the front: Hold the first bag piece over the strip with the wrong sides together so the bottom right corner of the bag meets the seam of the strip (A). Fasten on and ch 1. Sc the bottom of the bag to the strip, beginning each stitch by inserting your hook through the next stitch on the bag and the strip.

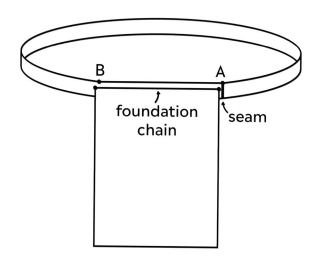

At the corner of the bag (B), make a second sc into the *same* corner of the bag and the *next* stitch of the strip. Turn your work so you can crochet the side of the bag to the strip.

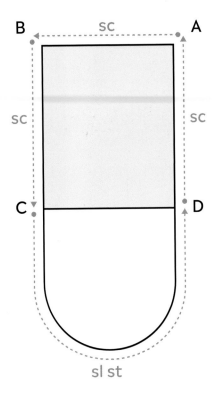

Match the side edge of the bag to the strip and hold in place with stitch markers if desired. Sc the pieces together from B to C. (I crocheted 3 sc into each right-side row of the bag edge and 2 sc into each wrong-side row. If your gauge is different, you might need more or fewer stitches to smoothly join the bag to the strip.)

To make the two sides match perfectly, pause at this stage and count how many stitches of the strip you matched to the side of the bag. From the starting point (A), count the same number of stitches along the strip edge in the opposite direction and mark this stitch (D) with a stitch marker.

Start crocheting again: Drop the bag and sl st along the edge of the strip to the marked stitch. At the marked stitch (D), hold the other corner of the bag over the strip and begin to sc through the bag and the strip again to form the final side seam, making the final stitch into the same corner stitch of the bag and the last stitch of the strip.

Join to the first stitch of the seam with a sl st (or use an invisible finish for a smoother join).

Fasten off and weave in the ends.

The slip stitches that run around the edge of the strap aren't just decoration—the inelastic edge they create, together with the nonstretchy foundation chain running through the middle, stops the strap from stretching when you use your bag.

Join the back: Turn the bag over, and along the other long edge of the strip, mark the stitches that correspond to the four corners of the bag front with stitch markers.

Place the second bag piece over the strip with the wrong sides together, matching the bag corners to the marked stitches, and repeat the joining instructions to crochet the back of the bag to the other edge of the strip.

Weave in all remaining yarn ends.

Resizing the Pattern

This bag is formed from two basic rectangles and a long strip, so it's easy to make a bag of any size. Just modify the starting chain and the number of rows as follows.

Bag width: ch any number for the bag front/back to give the desired width (plus 3 for the turning chain).

Bag height: Work as many rows as needed to give the desired height.

Strap length: The strap and gusset are worked as a single strip, so make your starting chain long enough to run down one side of the bag, across the bottom, and up the other side, plus your desired strap length.

Double Diagonals
Shawl

You stitch this showstopper
shawl from the bottom tip and
work upward from there, which
means you can keep crocheting
until you decide it's large
enough—or until you run out
of yarn! The versatile shallow
triangle shape is perfect to wear
as a stunning lacy scarf as well as
a shawl. The reduced depth also
means you can complete it faster
than a classic half-square
triangular shawl.

Measurements

About 62 inches (157cm) wide and 26 inches (66cm) tall, after blocking.

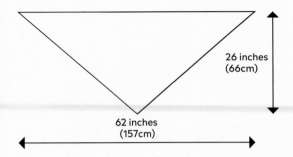

62 inches
(157cm)

26 inches
(66cm)

Yarn

About 460 yards (420m) fingering weight yarn (or quantity as desired to make a smaller/larger shawl). Shown in Knit Picks Capretta, 80% merino wool, 10% cashmere, 10% nylon.

Gauge

5 rows = 4 inches (10cm) and 5 stitch pattern repeats = 9 inches (23cm), after blocking. Gauge isn't at all important for this project. A different gauge will affect the final dimensions of the shawl, but you can keep adding more rows until the shawl is the desired size.

Note that crocheted lace will stretch considerably when blocked. My shawl grew by about 20% in each direction during blocking.

Hook

U.S. J/10 (6mm)

Other Supplies

Yarn needle, scissors, rustproof pins, blocking wires (optional), towel, surface for blocking

Notes

Lace patterns like this use a much larger hook than you'd usually use with fine yarn. The large hook makes the lace flow and drape beautifully.

If you plan to crochet until you run out of yarn, keep in mind you'll need to keep back about 10% of your yarn for the final row and border.

Special Stitches

Triple (treble) three together (tr3tog): *YO twice, insert hook into next st and draw up a loop, (YO and draw through 2 loops on hook) twice; rep from * 2 more times, YO and draw through all 4 loops on hook.

Picot: ch 3, sl st into front loop and left vertical bar of sc at base of ch.

Stitch Diagrams

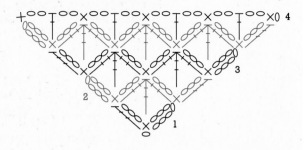

The first 3 rows of the shawl, one more repeat of Row 3, and the final row (Row 4).

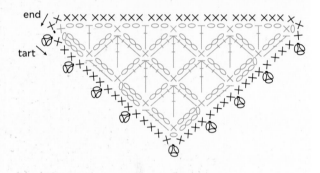

The border around a reduced sample of the shawl.

Double Diagonals Shawl

Ch 8.

Row 1: (sc, ch 3, tr) in 8th ch from hook.

Row 2: ch 7 (counts as tr + ch 3, here and throughout), turn, sc in same st (at base of ch), ch 3, tr3tog over same st, next sc and 4th ch of t-ch, ch 3, (sc, ch 3, tr) in same ch.

Row 3: ch 7, turn, *sc in same st, ch 3, tr3tog over same st, next sc and next tr3tog, ch 3; rep from * across to end, making last leg of final tr3tog into 4th ch of t-ch, (sc, ch 3, tr) in same ch.

Repeat Row 3 an additional 31 times or until the shawl reaches the desired dimensions.

Row 4: ch 1, turn, sc in 1st st, ch 2, dc in next sc, *ch 2, sc in next tr3tog, ch 2, dc in next sc; rep from * across to t-ch sp, ch 2, sc in 4th ch of t-ch.

Edging: Don't turn; to keep the instructions concise, treat the ch3-sp at the start of each row as the post of a tr st.

Work down the first side:

Picot, 3 sc around post of next tr, *picot, sc in edge of next sc, 3 sc around post of next tr**; rep from * to ** across to bottom tip, (sc, picot, sc) in base of ch at bottom tip.

Rotate the shawl to work up the other side:

3 sc around post of next tr, rep from * to ** up to top corner, picot, 3 sc in corner sc to turn corner.

Work along the top:

3 sc in each ch2-sp along top edge, 2 sc in last sc, sl st in same st.

Fasten off.

Wet block the shawl to open the lace pattern: Pin it out to dry in its triangular shape, ensuring all 3 edges are straight. For a step-by-step tutorial, see "Wet Blocking" on page 132. When completely dry, remove the pins and weave in the yarn ends.

Front-and-Back
Hat

Working into only alternating front and back loops gives this hat a beautiful, subtle texture and stretch. The front-and-back motif is echoed in the brim, which you create by working in front and back post stitches.

As well as complete patterns for child-sized and small and large adult sizes, these instructions include bonus measure-as-you-go directions for all sizes. Feel free to substitute a different yarn and hook combination that doesn't meet the specified gauge.

Measurements

To fit child (adult small, adult large), about 18 (20, 22) inches (45 [50, 55]cm) around and 6½ (7½, 8½) inches (16.5 [19, 21.5]cm) tall.

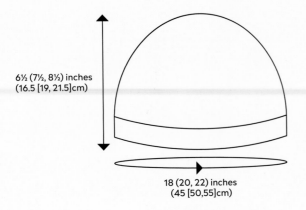

6½ (7½, 8½) inches
(16.5 [19, 21.5]cm)

18 (20, 22) inches
(45 [50,55]cm)

Yarn

About 95 (120, 150) yards (85 [110, 135]m) DK (light) weight yarn. Shown in Knit Picks Gloss DK, 70% merino wool, 30% silk.

Gauge

11 rows and 16 sts = 4 inches (10cm) in alternating (hdcFL, hdcBL) pattern. You don't have to meet gauge to make this hat (although this will affect the quantity of yarn required to make each size); you can instead measure as you go and work the number of rounds needed in your gauge to meet the stated measurements.

Hooks

U.S. H/8 (5mm), U.S. I/9 (5.5mm)

Other Supplies

Stitch marker, yarn needle, scissors

Notes

For a good fit, select the size that's about 1 inch (3cm) smaller than the circumference of your head just above your ears.

This pattern is worked in a continuous spiral and the stitch pattern is difficult to "read," so it's vitally important to use a stitch marker to mark the first stitch of each round. Otherwise, if you lose your place, it will be almost impossible to figure out where you are.

The stitch pattern might look a little crumpled as you crochet, but gently stretch out the stitches every few rounds and they'll relax into an even texture.

Special Stitches

hdcFL: half double crochet in front loop only.

hdcBL: half double crochet in back loop only.

FBinc: hdcFL in next st, hdcBL in *same* st.

Stitch Diagram

A sample of the main stitch pattern and the brim.

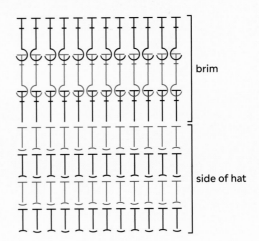

brim

side of hat

Front-and-Back Hat

Top:

Instead of trying to meet gauge, if you prefer, you can continue these increase rows until the top measures the desired diameter and then move on to the sides of the hat. The top will be slightly domed, so lay it on a table and smooth it out flat to measure the diameter:

Child: 6 inches (15cm)

Adult small: 6½ inches (16.5cm)

Adult large: 7 inches (18cm)

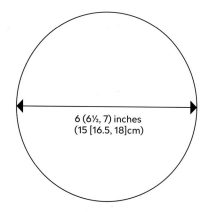

6 (6½, 7) inches
(15 [16.5, 18]cm)

With larger hook, make a magic ring, ch 1.

Rnd 1: (sc, 7 hdc) in magic ring. (8 sts) Pull the ring tightly closed.

Don't join at the end of the round; you'll be working in a continuous spiral and the 1st st of Rnd 2 should be made into the sc from the start of Rnd 1.

Rnd 2: FBinc in next 8 sts. (16 sts)

Rnd 3: *FBinc in next st, hdcFL in next st; rep from * around. (24 sts)

Rnd 4: *FBinc in next st, hdcFL in next st, hdcBL in next st; rep from * around. (32 sts)

Rnd 5: *FBinc in next st, hdcFL in next st, hdcBL in next st, hdcFL in next st; rep from * around. (40 sts)

Rnd 6: *FBinc in next st, (hdcFL in next st, hdcBL in next st) twice; rep from * around. (48 sts)

Rnd 7: *FBinc in next st, (hdcFL in next st, hdcBL in next st) twice, hdcFL in next st; rep from * around. (56 sts)

Rnd 8: *FBinc in next st, (hdcFL in next st, hdcBL in next st) 3 times; rep from * around. (64 sts)

Rnd 9: *FBinc in next st, (hdcFL in next st, hdcBL in next st) 3 times, hdcFL in next st; rep from * around. (72 sts)

Adult sizes only:

Rnd 10: *FBinc in next st, (hdcFL in next st, hdcBL in next st) 4 times; rep from * around. (80 sts)

Adult large size only:

Rnd 11: *FBinc in next st, (hdcFL in next st, hdcBL in next st) 4 times, hdcFL in next st; rep from * around. (88 sts)

Don't fasten off.

Sides:

When you reach the desired diameter, FBinc in next st and start to work (hdcFL in next st, hdcBL in next st) around in a continuous spiral. (73 [81, 89] sts) Don't stop at the end of each round. You can continue to mark rounds or lose the marker and just go by length by using the following measurements.

Continue in the alternating (hdcFL, hdcBL) stitch pattern for a total of 6 (8, 10) rounds or until the hat measures as follows (from the tip of the crown):

Child: 5½ inches (14cm)

Adult small: 6½ inches (16.5cm)

Adult large: 7½ inches (19cm)

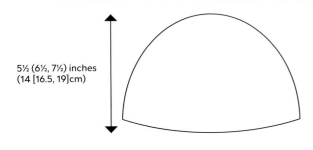

5½ (6½, 7½) inches
(14 [16.5, 19]cm)

If your last stitch was a hdcFL, hdcBL in next st.

Sc in FL of next st, sl st in BL of next st.

Don't fasten off.

Brim:

The brim is worked in joined rounds with the smaller hook. Work into both loops from now on.

Rnd 1: with smaller hook, ch 2 (counts as dc), dc in both loops of same st (the st you worked the sl st into), dc in each remaining st around. Join with sl st to top of ch 2. (74 [82, 90] sts)

Rnd 2: ch 2 (counts as BPdc), FPdc in next st, *BPdc in next st, FPdc in next st; rep from * around. Join with sl st to top of ch 2. (74 [82, 90] sts)

Rnd 3: ch 2 (counts as BPdc), FPdc in next st, *BPdc in next st, FPdc in next st; rep from * around. Join with sl st to top of ch 2 (or use an invisible finish for a smoother join). (74 [82, 90] sts)

Fasten off and weave in the ends.

Front-and-Back
Fingerless Mitts

Fingerless mitts (or wrist warmers) are the perfect way to keep your hands warm on chilly days while still leaving your fingers free to type, write, or crochet! Make a matching set by pairing these with the Front-and-Back Hat (page 250).

Measurements

To fit adult small (large), about 6¾ (7¾) inches (17 [20]cm) around and 7 inches (18cm) long.

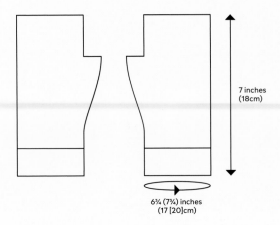

7 inches
(18cm)

6¾ (7¾) inches
(17 [20]cm)

Yarn

About 105 (120) yards (95 [110]m) DK (light) weight yarn. Shown in Knit Picks Gloss DK, 70% merino wool, 30% silk.

Gauge

11 rows and 16 sts = 4 inches (10cm) in alternating (hdcFL, hdcBL) pattern

Hooks

U.S. H/8 (5mm), U.S. I/9 (5.5mm)

Other Supplies

Stitch marker, yarn needle, scissors

Notes

These mitts are stretchy, so the two sizes should fit most women's hands. If you meet gauge but want to make your mitts a little larger or smaller, go up (or down) a hook size.

This pattern is worked in a continuous spiral and the stitch pattern is difficult to "read," so it's vitally important you use a stitch marker to note the first stitch of each round. Otherwise, if you lose your place, it will be almost impossible to figure out where you were.

The stitch pattern might look a little crumpled as you crochet, but gently stretch out the stitches every few rounds and they'll relax into an even texture as you continue.

Special Stitches

Foundation double crochet (fdc):

1st fdc: ch 3 (doesn't count as st), YO, insert hook into 3rd ch from hook and draw up a loop, YO and draw through 1 loop on hook (to form the ch), [YO and draw through 2 loops on hook] twice (to form the dc). (1 fdc completed)

Subsequent fdcs: work each st under the 2 loops that form the ch at the bottom of the previous st. YO, insert hook under both loops of the ch, draw up a loop, YO and draw through 1 loop on hook (to form the ch), [YO and draw through 2 loops on hook] twice (to form the dc).

hdcFL: half double crochet in front loop only.

hdcBL: half double crochet in back loop only.

FBinc: hdcFL in next st, hdcBL in same st.

Stitch Diagram

A sample of the cuff and the main stitch pattern.

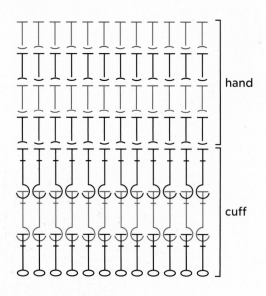

hand

cuff

Front-and-Back Fingerless Mitts

Make 2.

Cuff:

With smaller hook, leave an 8-inch (20cm) starting tail and fdc 26 (30). Join with sl st to top of 1st fdc, taking care not to twist your sts. (26 [30] sts)

Rnds 1 and 2: ch 2 (counts as BPdc), FPdc in next st, *BPdc in next st, FPdc in next st; rep from * around. Join with sl st to top of ch 2. (26 [30] sts)

Hand:

From this point on, you use the larger hook to work in a continuous spiral in an alternating (hdcFL, hdcBL) stitch pattern without joining between rounds. Don't forget to use a stitch marker in the first stitch of each round so you don't lose your place.

Rnd 3: with larger hook, ch 1, sc2tog in FL of 1st 2 sts, *hdcBL in next st, hdcFL in next st; rep from * around. (25 [29] sts)

Rnd 4: hdcBL in next st, *hdcFL in next st, hdcBL in next st; rep from * around. (25 [29] sts)

Rnd 5: hdcFL in next st, *hdcBL in next st, hdcFL in next st; rep from * around. (25 [29] sts)

Rnd 6: rep Round 4. (25 [29] sts)

Begin increases for the thumb gusset:

Rnd 7: FBinc in next 2 sts, hdcFL in next st, *hdcBL in next st, hdcFL in next st; rep from * around. (27 [31] sts)

Rnd 8: hdcBL in next st, FBinc in next 2 sts, *hdcFL in next st, hdcBL in next st; rep from * around. (29 [33] sts)

Rnd 9: hdcFL in next st, hdcBL in next st, FBinc in next 2 sts, hdcFL in next st, *hdcBL in next st, hdcFL in next st; rep from * around. (31 [35] sts)

Rnd 10: hdcBL in next st, hdcFL in next st, hdcBL in next st, FBinc in next 2 sts, *hdcFL in next st, hdcBL in next st; rep from * around. (33 [37] sts)

Rnd 11: (hdcFL in next st, hdcBL in next st) twice, FBinc in next 2 sts, hdcFL in next st, *hdcBL in next st, hdcFL in next st; rep from * around. (35 [39] sts)

Rnd 12: hdcBL in next st, *hdcFL in next st, hdcBL in next st; rep from * around. (35 [39] sts)

Rnd 13: hdcFL in next st, *hdcBL in next st, hdcFL in next st; rep from * around. (35 [39] sts)

Rnd 14: *hdcBL in next st, hdcFL in next st; rep from * around to last st, hdcBL in next st, hdcFL in *same* st. (36 [40] sts)

Leave the thumb hole and continue with the hand:

Rnd 15: sk next 10 sts, hdcBL in next st, hdcFL in same st, hdcBL in next st, *hdcFL in next st, hdcBL in next st; rep from * around. (27 [31] sts)

Rnd 16: hdcFL in next st, *hdcBL in next st, hdcFL in next st; rep from * around. (27 [31] sts)

Rnd 17: hdcBL in next st, *hdcFL in next st, hdcBL in next st; rep from * around. (27 [31] sts)

Rnd 18: rep Round 16. (27 [31] sts)

Rnd 19: sc in BL of next st, sl st in next st. (2 sts, plus 25 [29] unworked)

Fasten off (if desired, use an invisible finish in the next stitch to create a smoother join) and weave in the yarn tail.

Use the long starting tail and a yarn needle to stitch closed the gap at the base of the cuff, hiding the starting ch 3 from the chainless foundation on the inside of the cuff. Weave in the remaining yarn tail.

Left-Handed Reference

Holding Your Hook and Yarn

There's no single correct method for holding your crochet hook and yarn. With time, you'll discover the method that works best for you. The most important thing is that you're comfortable. If you feel any discomfort or pain, try a different hold or position until you find one that feels natural to you.

Holding Your Hook

The two most common ways to hold a crochet hook are the *overhand* (or *knife*) grip and the *underhand* or (*pencil*) grip. For either grip, grasp the hook's thumb rest between the thumb and index finger of your left hand so the throat of the hook faces you.

For the knife grip, place your hand over the hook and support the handle against your palm with your remaining fingers, as if you're holding a knife.

For the pencil grip, let the handle of the hook rest on top of your hand, as if you're holding a pencil.

Holding Your Yarn

Your right hand also plays an important part in your crocheting: It controls the tension in your yarn, which influences how tight your stitches are. You can wrap the yarn over and around your fingers in any number of ways. Here are two of the most common.

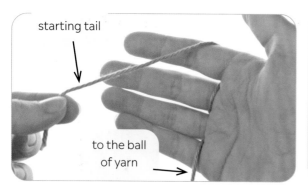

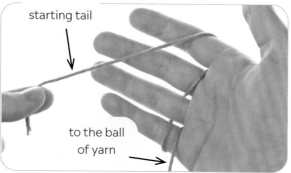

With your right palm facing you and the end of the yarn in your left hand, pass the yarn in front of your little finger, behind your ring finger, in front of your middle finger, and behind your index finger.

With your right palm facing you and the end of the yarn in your left hand, bring the yarn over and around your little finger in a complete loop and then pass the yarn behind your ring finger, in front of your middle finger, and behind your index finger.

Your right hand will stay busy as you crochet. You'll also hold your work steady between your right thumb and middle finger.

Whichever option you choose, when you have the yarn wrapped through your fingers, close your hand gently around the yarn so your palm faces down. The yarn should be able to slide through your fingers without chafing your hand but not so freely that the working yarn goes slack. Keeping the yarn taut as you work helps keep your stitches neat and even.

Making a Slipknot

To begin crocheting, you need to attach your yarn to your hook with a slipknot.

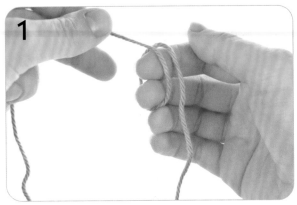

Leaving a 6-inch (15cm) tail of yarn hanging down over your right hand, lay the yarn over one or two fingertips and take it around them to form a loop.

Remove your fingers from the loop, holding it in place between your thumb and a fingertip, and insert your hook into the loop.

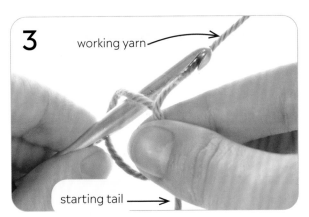

working yarn

starting tail

Catch the working yarn with your hook. (The working yarn is the yarn that heads to the yarn ball, not the short starting tail.)

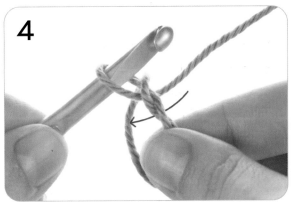

Use the hook to pull the yarn up through the loop.

5

Pull on the yarn ends to tighten the knot.

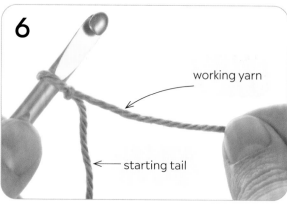

6

working yarn

starting tail

Pull the working yarn to draw the loop closed around your hook.

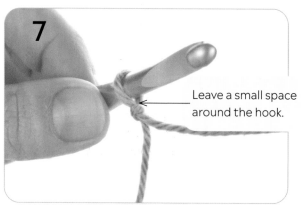

7

Leave a small space around the hook.

Leave the loop loose enough that your hook can easily slide up and down inside it.

If you find you need to pull on the starting tail instead of the working yarn to tighten the slipknot around your hook, you've made an adjustable slipknot (a knot that can loosen itself). You need a secure knot to start your crochet, so if you've accidentally made an adjustable slipknot, undo it and start again.

Making a Yarn Over

A *yarn over* (YO) is one of the most essential moves in crochet. Although it might sound like you wrap the yarn around the hook with your right hand, it's quicker and easier to keep your right hand still and use your hook to grab the yarn.

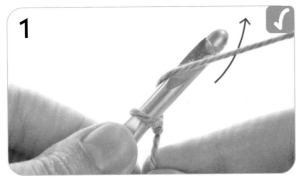

Pass your hook underneath the yarn so the yarn lies over the hook. The working yarn (that heads to your right hand) is on the right side of the hook.

Do not pass the hook over the yarn and catch it from above so the working yarn is on the left side of the hook. This would twist your stitches.

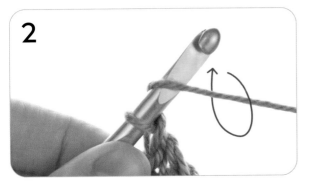

To yarn over twice, swing the hook over and back under the yarn again in the same direction.

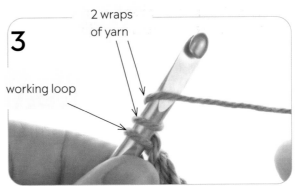

You now have 3 loops on your hook: the working loop and the yarn wrapped twice around the hook.

Drawing Up a Loop

All crochet stitches are formed by inserting your hook into a previous stitch and pulling a new loop through that stitch. This process is called *drawing up a loop*.

Insert your hook into the next stitch.

Yarn over. To draw up a loop, reverse the path of your hook, so you pull the hook back out of the stitch, drawing the yarn with it.

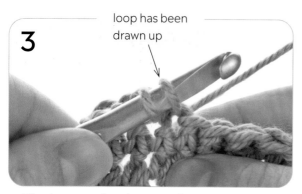

loop has been drawn up

The loop you've drawn up is now on your hook, along with the loop you started with.

If you see "insert hook in next stitch and draw up a loop" or "draw up a loop in the next stitch" written in a pattern, that means the yarn over is implied. You can't draw up a loop without first catching the yarn with your hook.

Making a Foundation Chain

The *foundation chain* runs along the bottom of your crocheted piece and provides a base into which you work your stitches.

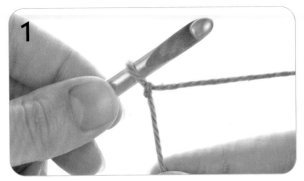

Start with a slipknot on your hook.

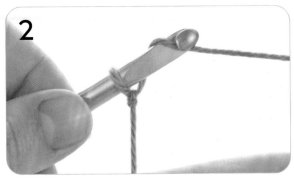

Yarn over.

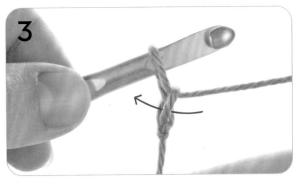

Draw your hook back through the loop already on your hook.

You now have 1 chain (abbreviated *ch*).

To make it easier to draw the yarn through your stitches, rotate the hook toward you after you yarn over. With the head of the hook facing sideways, it's less likely to catch on your stitches.

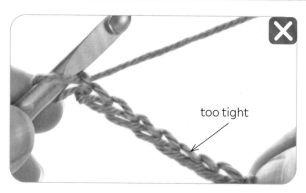

too tight

Repeat steps 2 and 3 for each additional chain. To help support the chain as you pull your hook through, hold on to the stitches you've already chained with your right hand. Move your hand up the chain every few stitches so you always hold the chain close to your hook.

It will take some practice to make your chains look consistent. Although a loose chain might look untidy, resist the urge to neaten your chain stitches by pulling on the yarn to shrink the stitch. This would tighten the stitch into a knot, which isn't what you want. A crocheted chain must be loose and open so you can insert your hook back into each chain loop without a struggle.

Counting Chains

If you look at your chain, the front of the chain—the side that faces you as you crochet—should look like a row of Vs. Each of these Vs is one chain stitch. When you count your chains, start from the V above the slipknot and count each V up to your hook. The loop on your hook is called the *working loop*. **Do not** count this as a stitch.

To make it easier to keep count when you're making a long foundation chain, mark every 10 or 20 chains with a stitch marker.

If in doubt, especially with a long starting chain, add a few extra chains to ensure you have enough. You can easily unravel the extras after you complete the first row if you have too many. However, if you have too few, you'd have to unravel the entire first row to add the additional chains.

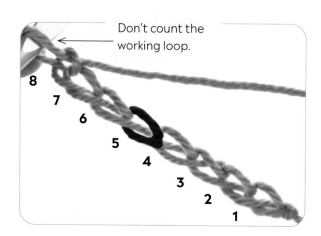

Don't count the working loop.

Working into the Foundation Chain

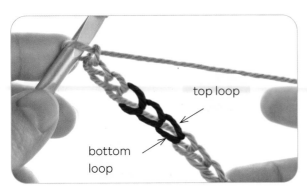

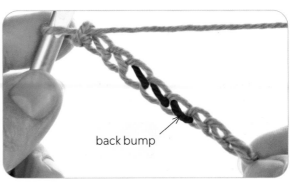

Look at the front side of your foundation chain and you'll see it looks like a row of sideways Vs. Each V is made of two loops: the *top loop* and the *bottom loop*.

If you turn over the foundation chain, you'll see a line of bumps along the back. These are called the *back bumps* of the chain.

There's no one correct way to insert your hook into a chain. The most important thing is to be consistent and insert your hook into the same part of the chain to begin each stitch. The following sections show the most common ways to work into a chain.

Under the Top Loop

In this method, you hook under the top loop only.

Here, the hook is inserted under the top loop only.

Under the Top Loop and Back Bump

In this method, you hook under both the top loop and the back bump. This is sometimes referred to as the *top 2 loops* of the chain.

Here, the hook is inserted under the top loop and the back bump.

Under the Back Bump

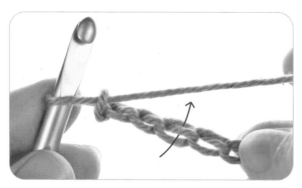

In this method, you turn over the chain and insert your hook under the back bump of each chain.

Here, the chain has been turned over and the hook is inserted under the back bump.

Which should you use? Working into the top loop only is the easiest method for beginners and the way the stitches in this book are made unless otherwise noted, but it makes a loose edge with large holes. After you've gained some confidence with making crochet stitches, I recommend working into the back bumps of the chain (unless a pattern specifies otherwise) because it makes a strong, neat edge. The stitch demonstrations in Chapter 3 are all worked in the easiest way: into the top loop of the chain.

Working into Subsequent Rows

Standard crochet stitches are worked from left to right, so when you reach the end of a row, you turn your work so you can work from left to right across the top of the row you just completed.

Before turning your work, you'll make a *turning chain* to bring your hook and yarn up to the height of the next row. The number of stitches in your turning chain depends on the stitches you're making. (See "Turning Chains" on page 48 for more details.)

back loop

front loop

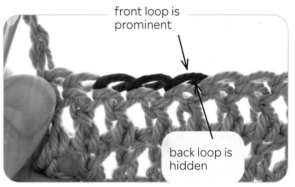

front loop is prominent

back loop is hidden

After turning your work, look at the top of the row you've just completed. The top of each stitch looks like a sideways V—similar to the front of a chain stitch. Each V is made of two loops: the *front loop* (the loop closest to you) and the *back loop* (the loop farthest from you).

Tilt your work forward so you can clearly see the Vs along the top of the row. If you look straight at your work from the front (as shown above), you only see the front loops of the stitches because the back loops are lower and farther back.

Under the Front and Back Loops

Unless otherwise specified in a pattern, the standard way to work into a crochet stitch is by inserting your hook under both the front and back loops of the stitch in the previous row.

Here, the hook is inserted under both the front and back loops.

Under the Front Loops Only

If a pattern specifies that your stitches are worked in *front loops only,* insert your hook under just the front loop.

Here, the hook is inserted into only the front loop of the stitch.

Under the Back Loops Only

If a pattern specifies that your stitches are worked in *back loops only,* insert your hook under just the back loop.

Here, the hook is inserted into only the back loop of the stitch.

If a pattern doesn't specify which loop(s) to work into, insert your hook under both loops of the stitch below. If you work into only one loop, the unworked loops form a horizontal ridge along the base of every row.

Single Crochet

Single crochet (abbreviated *sc*) is the most basic crochet stitch—and the easiest one to learn.

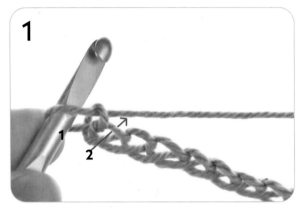

Make a foundation chain of the required number of stitches plus 1. Identify the second chain from your hook.

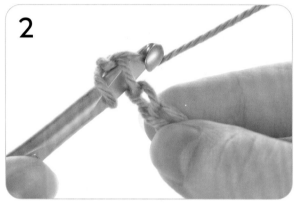

Insert your hook into the second chain from your hook and yarn over.

Draw up a loop. This leaves you with 2 loops on your hook.

Yarn over and draw the yarn through both loops on the hook to complete the stitch. This leaves you with 1 loop on your hook.

5

Complete the first row of single crochet stitches by repeating steps 2 through 4 into each remaining chain. At the end of the row, chain 1.

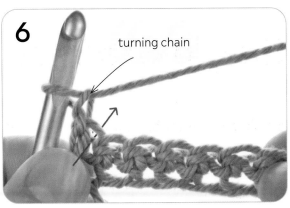

6

turning chain

Turn your work and identify the first stitch of the row.

7

Insert your hook under both loops of the stitch and yarn over.

8

Repeat steps 3 and 4 to complete the stitch.

At the end of each row of sc, remember that the turning chain **does not** count as a stitch. Don't stitch into it or your work will get one stitch wider with every row.

Glossary

asterisk * A symbol used to mark a point in a pattern row, usually the beginning of a set of repeated instructions.

back loop (BL) only A method of crocheting in which you work into only the back loop of a stitch instead of both loops.

back post (BP) stitches Textured stitches worked from the back around the post of the stitch below.

ball band The paper wrapper around a ball of yarn that contains such information as fiber content, amount/length of yarn, weight, color, and dye lot.

block A finishing technique that uses moisture to set your stitches and shape pieces to their final measurements.

blocking wire A long, straight wire used to hold the edges of crochet pieces straight during blocking, most often for lace.

bobble A combination crochet stitch that stands out from the fabric, formed from several incomplete tall stitches joined at the top and bottom.

brackets [ ] Symbols used to surround a set of grouped instructions; often used to indicate repeats.

chain (ch) A simple crochet stitch that often forms the foundation other stitches are worked into.

chain space (ch-sp) A gap formed beneath one or more chain stitches; usually worked into instead of into the individual chain(s).

chainless foundation A stretchy foundation plus the first row of stitches that are made in one step.

chainless foundation stitches Stitches that have an extra chain at the bottom so they can be worked into without first crocheting a foundation chain.

chart A visual depiction of a crochet pattern that uses symbols to represent stitches.

cluster A combination stitch formed from several incomplete tall stitches, joined together at the top.

contrast color (CC) A yarn color used as an accent to the project's main color.

crochet hook The tool used to form all crochet stitches; available in various sizes, styles, and materials.

crossed stitches Two or more tall stitches that are crossed, one in front of the other, to create an X shape.

decrease (dec) A shaping technique in which you reduce the number of stitches in your work.

double crochet (dc) A basic stitch twice as tall as a single crochet stitch.

drape The way in which your crocheted fabric hangs; how stiff or flowing it feels.

draw up a loop To pull up a loop of yarn through a stitch or space after inserting your hook into that stitch or space.

fan   A group of several tall stitches, crocheted into the same base stitch and usually separated by chains, that forms a fan shape.

fasten off   To lock the final stitch with the yarn end so the crocheted work can't unravel.

fasten on   To draw up a loop of new yarn through a stitch in preparation to begin crocheting with it.

foundation chain   A base chain into which most crochet is worked (unless worked in the round).

foundation stitches, chainless   See chainless foundation stitches.

fringe   A decorative edging made from strands of yarn knotted along the edge.

frog   To unravel your crochet work by removing your hook and pulling the working yarn.

front loop (FL) only   A method of crocheting in which you work into only the front loop of a stitch instead of both loops.

front post (FP) stitches   Textured stitches worked from the front around the post of the stitch below.

gauge   A measure of how many stitches and rows fit into a certain length of crocheted fabric, usually 4 inches (10cm), that indicates the size of each stitch.

granny square   A classic motif created from groups of double crochet stitches separated by chain spaces.

half double crochet (hdc)   A basic stitch halfway between the height of a single and double crochet stitch.

increase (inc)   A shaping technique in which you add extra stitches to your work.

invisible finish   A method of finishing a round or edging so the join isn't visible.

knife grip   An overhand method of holding a crochet hook, similar to holding a knife.

linked stitch   A variation of any standard tall stitch that links the stitch to its neighbor partway up the post to eliminate the gaps between stitches and form a solid fabric.

magic ring   A technique to begin working in the round, without leaving a hole in the center, by crocheting over an adjustable loop.

main color (MC)   The predominant yarn color of a crocheted piece.

mattress stitch   A stitch to sew a seam that forms an almost invisible join on the right side of the work and a ridged seam on the wrong side.

motif   A crocheted shape, usually worked in the round as a geometric shape and combined with other motifs into larger pieces.

parentheses ( )   Symbols used to surround a set of grouped instructions; often used to indicate repeats.

pencil grip   An underhand method of holding a crochet hook, similar to holding a pencil.

picot   A tiny loop of chain stitches that sits on top of a stitch and creates a small round or pointed shape.

popcorn   A combination stitch that stands out dramatically from the fabric, formed from several tall stitches pulled together by a chain stitch.

post   The main vertical stem of a stitch.

post stitch   A stitch formed by crocheting around the post of the stitch in the row or round below so the stitch sits in front of (or behind) the surface of the fabric.

puff stitch   A combination crochet stitch that forms a smooth, puffy shape created from several incomplete half double crochet stitches that are joined at the top and bottom.

repeat (rep)   To replicate a series of crochet instructions; one instance of the duplication.

reverse single crochet (rsc)   A variation of single crochet that's worked backward (left to right) around the edge of a piece, producing a corded edging.

right side (RS)   The side of a crocheted piece that will be visible; the outside or front.

rip back   To unravel your work by removing your hook and pulling the working yarn.

round (rnd)   A line of stitches worked around a circular crocheted piece.

row   A line of stitches worked across a flat crocheted piece.

shell   A group of several tall stitches, crocheted into the same base stitch, that spread out at the top into a shell shape.

single crochet (sc)   The most basic and common crochet stitch.

skip (sk)   To pass over a stitch or stitches and not work into it or them.

slipknot   A knot that can be tightened by pulling one end of the yarn; used for attaching the yarn to the hook to begin crocheting.

slip stitch (sl st)   A stitch with no height primarily used to join rounds and stitches or to move the hook and yarn to a new position.

space (sp)   A gap formed between or beneath stitches; often seen in lace patterns.

spike stitch   A stitch worked around existing stitches to extend down to one or more rows below, creating a long vertical spike of yarn.

stash   A collection of accumulated yarn.

stitch (st)   A group of one or more loops of yarn pulled through each other in a specified order until only one loop remains on the hook.

stitch diagram   A map of a crochet or stitch pattern that looks similar to the finished piece, with each stitch represented by a symbol.

stitch marker   A small tool you can slide into a crochet stitch or between stitches to mark a position.

swatch   A crocheted sample of a stitch pattern large enough to measure the gauge and test the pattern with a specific hook and yarn.

tail   *See yarn tail.*

together (tog)   A shaping technique in which you work two or more stitches into one to reduce the number of stitches.

triple (treble) crochet (tr)   A basic crochet stitch that's three times as tall as a single crochet stitch.

turning chain (t-ch)   A chain made at the start of a row to bring your hook and yarn up to the height of the next row.

V   The two loops at the top of each stitch that form a sideways V shape; standard crochet stitches are worked into both these loops.

V stitch   A group of two tall stitches crocheted into the same base stitch and separated by one or more chains, forming a V shape.

weave in   A method to secure and hide the yarn tails by stitching them through your crocheted stitches.

whip stitch   A simple stitch to sew a seam by inserting the needle through the edge of both crocheted pieces at once to form each stitch.

working in the round   Crocheting in a circle instead of backward and forward in straight rows.

working loop   The single loop that remains on your hook after completing a crochet stitch.

working yarn   The yarn coming from the ball that will form the next stitch.

wrong side (WS)   The side of a crocheted piece that will be hidden; the inside or back.

yardage   A length of yarn, usually expressed as an estimate of the amount of yarn required for a project.

yarn needle   A wide, blunt-tipped needle with an eye large enough for the yarn to pass through that's used for stitching crocheted pieces together and weaving in ends.

yarn over (YO)   To pass the yarn over the hook so the yarn is caught in the throat of the hook.

yarn tail   A short length of unworked yarn left at the start or end of a piece.

yarn weight   The thickness of the yarn (not the weight of a ball of yarn).

Quick
Reference

This table offers a quick reference for the standard crochet stitches, abbreviations, and chart symbols used in this book's project instructions.

Stitch Name	Abbreviation	Symbol	Description
back loop	BL		the loop farthest away from you at the top of the stitch
back post double crochet	BPdc		yarn over, insert the hook from the back to the front to the back around the post of the next stitch, yarn over and draw up a loop, (yarn over and draw through 2 loops) twice
chain(s)	ch(s)		yarn over and draw through the loop on the hook
chain space(s)	ch-sp(s)		the space beneath one or more chains
double crochet	dc		yarn over, insert the hook into the next stitch and draw up a loop, (yarn over and draw through 2 loops on the hook) twice
double crochet 2 together	dc2tog		(yarn over, insert the hook into the next stitch and draw up a loop, yarn over and draw through 2 loops on the hook) twice, yarn over and draw through all 3 loops on the hook
front loop	FL		the loop closest to you at the top of the stitch
front post double crochet	FPdc		yarn over, insert the hook from the front to the back to the front around the post of the next stitch, yarn over and draw up a loop, (yarn over and draw through 2 loops) twice

Stitch Name	Abbreviation	Symbol	Description
half double crochet	hdc	⊤	yarn over, insert the hook into the next stitch and draw up a loop, yarn over and draw through all 3 loops on the hook
repeat	rep		replicate a series of given instructions
single crochet	sc	× or +	insert the hook into the next stitch and draw up a loop, yarn over and draw through both loops on the hook
single crochet 2 together	sc2tog	⋏⋏	(insert the hook into the next stitch and draw up a loop) twice, yarn over and draw through all 3 loops on the hook
skip	sk		pass over a stitch or stitches; don't work into it
slip stitch	sl st	● or •	insert the hook into the next stitch, draw up a loop through the stitch and the loop on the hook
stitch(es)	st(s)		the basic building block of crochet; a group of one or more loops of yarn pulled through each other in a specified order until only 1 remains on the crochet hook
triple (treble) crochet	tr	⟊	yarn over twice, insert the hook into the next stitch and draw up a loop, (yarn over and draw through 2 loops on the hook) 3 times
turning chain	t-ch		the chain made at the start of a row to bring your hook and yarn up to the height of the next row
yarn over	YO		pass the yarn over the hook so the yarn is caught in the throat of the hook

Index

Publisher Mike Sanders
Art & Design Director William Thomas
Senior Editor Alexandra Andrzejewski
Editor Christopher Stolle
Cover Designer Lindsay Dobbs
Compositor Lissa Auciello-Brogan
Proofreaders Mary Anne Stolle & Jean Bissell
Indexer Tere Mullin

First American Edition, 2022
Published in the United States by DK Publishing
6081 E. 82nd St., Suite 400, Indianapolis, IN 46250

Published in the United States by Dorling Kindersley Limited.
Library of Congress Catalog Number: 2022934766
ISBN: 978-0-7440-6171-0

Note: This publication contains the opinions and ideas of its author. It is intended to provide
helpful and informative material on the subject matter covered. It is sold with the understanding
that the author and publisher are not engaged in rendering professional services in the book.
If the reader requires personal assistance or advice, a competent professional should be
consulted. The author and publisher specifically disclaim any responsibility for any liability,
loss, or risk, personal or otherwise, which is incurred as a consequence, directly or indirectly,
of the use and application of any of the contents of this book.

Trademarks: All terms mentioned in this book that are known to be or are suspected of being
trademarks or service marks have been appropriately capitalized. DK and Penguin Random
House LLC cannot attest to the accuracy of this information. Use of a term in this book
should not be regarded as affecting the validity of any trademark or service mark.

DK books are available at special discounts when purchased in bulk for sales promotions,
premiums, fund-raising, or educational use. For details, contact: SpecialSales@dk.com.

Printed and bound in China

Reprinted and updated from *Idiot's Guide: Crochet*

For the curious
www.dk.com